GEOGRAPHY

Regions

AUTHORS
James F. Marran
Social Studies Chair Emeritus
New Trier Township High School
Winnetka, Illinois

Cathy L. Salter
Geography Teacher
Educational Consultant
Hartsburg, Missouri

 **SRA
McGraw-Hill**
Columbus, Ohio

*A Division of The **McGraw·Hill** Companies*

Program Reviewers

Bonny Berryman
Eighth Grade Social Studies Teacher
Ramstad Middle School
Minot, North Dakota

Grace Foraker
Fourth Grade Teacher
B. B. Owen Elementary School
Lewisville Independent School District
Lewisville, Texas

Wendy M. Fries
Teacher/Visual and Performing Arts Specialist
Kings River Union School District
Tulare County, California

Maureen Maroney
Teacher
Horace Greeley I. S. 10 Queens
District 30
New York City, New York

Geraldeen Rude
Elementary Social Studies Teacher
1993 North Dakota Teacher of the Year
Minot Public Schools
Minot, North Dakota

SRA/McGraw-Hill

A Division of The **McGraw·Hill** *Companies*

Send all inquiries to:
SRA/McGraw-Hill
250 Old Wilson Bridge Road, Suite 310
Worthington, OH 43085

Printed in the United States of America.

ISBN 0-02-688163-2

4 5 6 7 8 9 POH 01 00 99

Table of Contents

Images of Earth

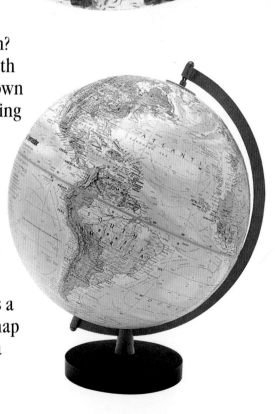

As you read about Earth, think about different ways that we can represent what Earth looks like.

Which one of these three images represents Earth? All of them! The first is an actual photograph of Earth taken from space. The blue areas are water. The brown areas are land. And the white areas are clouds floating above Earth.

The second picture shows a globe. Notice that the shape of the globe matches the shape of Earth shown in the photo taken from space. In this way, a globe represents Earth as it looks from space. A globe gives a more accurate image of Earth because it is shaped like Earth.

The third image shows a map of the world. A map is a flat drawing of some or all of Earth's surface. The map shows how the land is divided into continents. On a flat map, distances or directions can look different than they really are.

When we study geography, we need to be able to "see" Earth's surface. Of these three ways to represent Earth, maps are probably the most useful. A map can be folded up and easily carried around, unlike a globe. And, unlike a photo of Earth from space, a map can show details of Earth's surface. For example, different types of maps show us different things and can be used for different purposes. We might use a map to help us find a particular mountain, river, town, or city. Airplane pilots and ship captains use maps to find their way from place to place. Other types of maps can tell us about population, climate, cultures, or roads.

A map's title tells us what the map shows. Other features of a map may be represented in different colors. Still others may be represented by a symbol, such as a circle, dotted line, or road sign. Sometimes the meaning of the symbols is obvious. For example, a forest may be indicated by a tree. An airport's location might be shown with an illustration of an airplane. To make sure that everyone understands what the symbols mean, a mapmaker includes a legend, or key. This is a box that shows what each symbol or color represents.

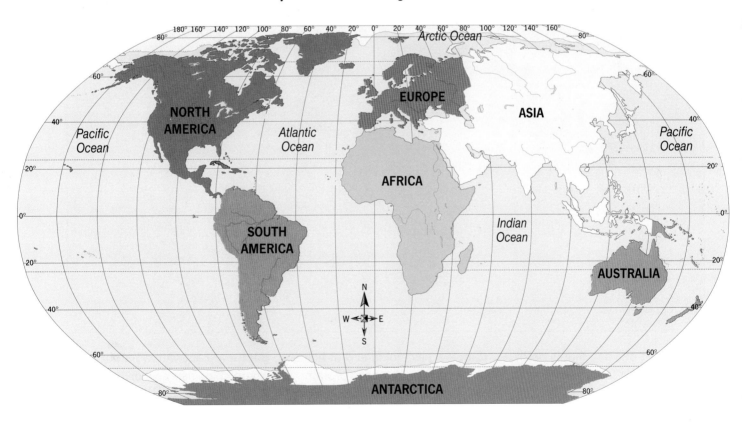

Look again at the images of Earth. Notice that two basic features make up the surface of Earth. They are large masses of land and even larger bodies of water. Do you know what these land masses and bodies of water are called? If you said continents and oceans, you're right!

3

Lesson 1
MAP SKILLS
Using a Map to Identify Different Forms of Land and Water

Words like mountain, river, or lake describe specific geographic features on Earth's surface. The map below shows and defines several types of landforms and water forms.

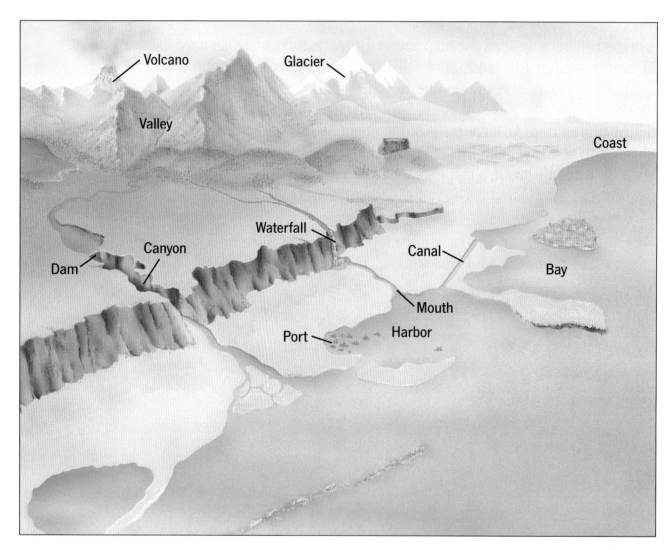

bay – part of a sea that is partly surrounded by land, smaller than a gulf

canal – a waterway built to carry water from one place to another

canyon – a deep, narrow valley that has steep sides

coast – land along the sea

dam – a piece of land that holds back the flow of a body of water

glacier – a huge mass of ice that slowly slides down a mountain

harbor – a deep body of water where ships can anchor

mouth – the place where a river empties into a larger body of water

port – a place with a harbor where ships can anchor

valley – the lower land that lies between hills and mountains

volcano – an opening in Earth's crust from which ashes and hot gases flow

waterfall – a stream that flows over the edge of a cliff

A. Read the definition of each word and look at its picture on the map. Notice that some words, such as *valley*, relate to land features. Some words, such as *bay*, relate to water.

1. Complete the chart below by writing the terms from the map in the appropriate column. An example has been done for you.

Land	Water
valley	bay

2. Under which of the above columns would you list continents? _____

3. Under which of the above columns would you list oceans? _____

B. Some of the different forms of land and water on Earth's surface are physical, or natural, features. Others are human-made features. Using the map and definitions shown, answer the following questions.

1. Which of the landforms and water forms are physical, or natural, features?

_____

2. Which ones are human-made features?

_____

3. Are there any that can be both formed by nature and made by humans?

_____

Lesson 1

ACTIVITY Identify land, water, natural, and human-made features.

Name That Feature

The **BIG**
Geographic Question

How can we learn to identify specific landforms and water forms?

In the article you read about the different ways Earth's land and water features can be represented. In the map skills lesson you learned the names of some specific land and water forms. Now create and play a game called "Name That Feature."

A. List the seven continents.

1. _____

2. _____

3. _____

4. _____

5. _____

6. _____

7. _____

B. List the four oceans.

1. _____

2. _____

3. _____

4. _____

C. Unscramble each set of letters below to write the names of landforms and water forms.

1. coolvan _____

2. trop _____

3. mad _____

4. aby _____

5. laacn _____

6. coats _____

7. houtm _____

8. tellarfaw _____

9. clearig _____

10. lavley _____

11. cannyo _____

12. borrah _____

D. Using index cards and all of the words you listed in steps A, B, and C, make cards for a "Name That Feature" game.

1. Make cards for each of the land and water features. On one side of the card, write the name and definition of the feature. On the reverse side of the card, draw a picture of the feature.

2. Make cards for the seven continents by drawing their shapes on one side of the card and writing their names on the reverse side.

3. Make cards for the four oceans by writing a description of the continents they are located near on one side of the card and writing their names on the reverse side.

E. Play the game by turning the picture-side of the cards face up and trying to name the feature. Turn the card over to check your accuracy. Challenge yourself by sorting all of the cards into land or water groups.

Lesson 2

States UNITED

As you read about the similarities and differences in various areas of our country, think about how people have grouped similar places to create regions.

The United States is the fourth-largest country in the world in area, and the third largest in population. The features that make up our country range from hot, sandy beaches to cold, snowy mountains, from level prairies to rolling countryside. There are deserts, canyons, rivers, and plains.

The natural resources of the United States are varied, also. Fertile farmland, thick forests, valuable minerals, and abundant sources of water help make our nation one of the richest countries in the world. Our human resources—the United States population—are also diverse. The people who live in the United States have different histories, cultures, and ways of earning a living.

In studying Earth's land and people, it is useful to identify and organize areas of Earth's surface in different ways. To do this, people have created **regions,** areas of land that share certain features that make them different from other areas. A region might be as small as a neighborhood or as large as a country.

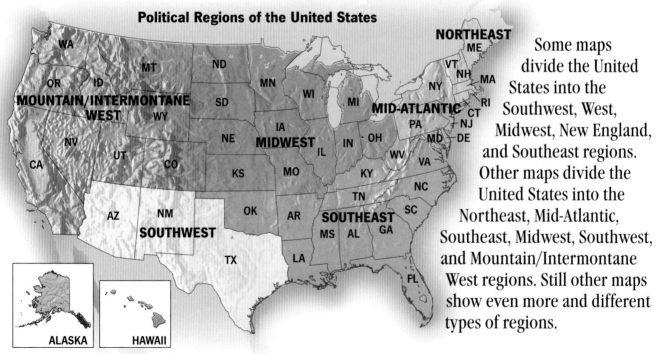

Political Regions of the United States

NORTHEAST

MOUNTAIN/INTERMONTANE WEST

MID-ATLANTIC

MIDWEST

SOUTHWEST

SOUTHEAST

ALASKA   HAWAII

Some maps divide the United States into the Southwest, West, Midwest, New England, and Southeast regions. Other maps divide the United States into the Northeast, Mid-Atlantic, Southeast, Midwest, Southwest, and Mountain/Intermontane West regions. Still other maps show even more and different types of regions.

This map shows one way the United States is divided into regions.

8

The two basic kinds of regions are *physical* and *human*. **Physical regions** are areas of the natural landscape that might be defined by their landforms, plant and animal life, natural resources, or climate. **Human regions** are based on characteristics of the area's people, such as their language or their government.

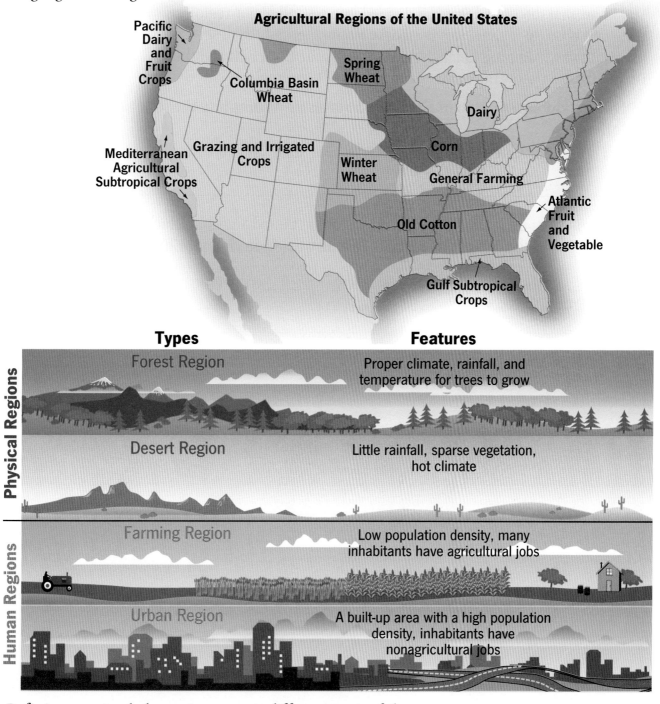

Agricultural Regions of the United States

Pacific Dairy and Fruit Crops

Columbia Basin Wheat

Spring Wheat

Dairy

Mediterranean Agricultural Subtropical Crops

Grazing and Irrigated Crops

Winter Wheat

Corn

General Farming

Atlantic Fruit and Vegetable

Old Cotton

Gulf Subtropical Crops

	Types	Features
Physical Regions	Forest Region	Proper climate, rainfall, and temperature for trees to grow
	Desert Region	Little rainfall, sparse vegetation, hot climate
Human Regions	Farming Region	Low population density, many inhabitants have agricultural jobs
	Urban Region	A built-up area with a high population density, inhabitants have nonagricultural jobs

Defining a region helps us to compare different parts of the United States and to understand what life is like there. It gives us a better picture of the physical and human features of an area. Can you see why creating regions is useful?

Lesson 2
MAP SKILLS
Using an Outline Map
to Create Regions

You know that the United States is divided into several major regions. Some are physical regions, like the Rocky Mountains and the deserts of the Southwest; some are human regions such as the Corn Belt and the Dixie. Maps can show the borders and names of these regions.

A. Look at the below map of the United States and complete the following.

1. Locate your state on the map and write your state name below.

_____

2. If you were describing the general area of the United States in which your state is located, which one of the following would you choose? Check one.

_____ the South _____ the North _____ the East _____ the West

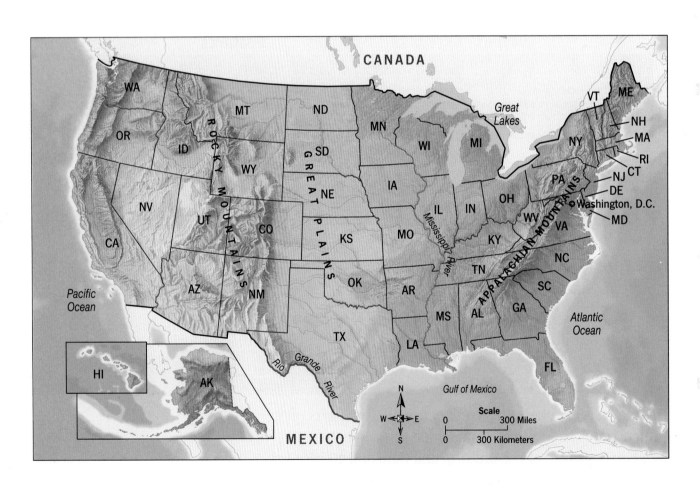

B. Think about where you live in the United States.

   1. Write the names of the states near your state that you think have similar features—such as beaches, mountains, forests, or weather—to your state.

   _____   _____

   _____   _____

   2. If you could give your state, together with the ones you listed above, a "region" name, what would you call the region? Think about features the states share and write a region name below.

   _____

C. Looking at the map, think about what you know about the different areas of our country. What makes each area special or unique? How would you divide the United States into regions?

   1. Write the names of the regions you would include.

   a. _____   **d.** _____

   b. _____   **e.** _____

   c. _____   **f.** _____

   2. Make notes about where you will draw the borders for each region.

   _____

   _____

   _____

   _____

D. Draw and label your regions on the map on page 10.

E. Compare your map with the regional maps in the article.

   1. Does your map have the same number of regions? _____

   2. Which, if any, borders are alike, and which are different? Why do you think the same or different borders were chosen?

   _____

   _____

Lesson 2

ACTIVITY   Identify features of regions.

What Makes Up a Region?

The BIG Geographic Question

What are the characteristics of different physical and human regions of the United States?

From the article you learned that there are different ways to divide the United States into regions. The map skills lesson allowed you to create your own regions. Now identify the characteristics of specific human and physical regions of the United States and explain the similarities that make them a region.

A. Use the information in the article and Almanac to help you brainstorm a list of different kinds of regions.

1. Write the names of as many physical regions as you can find. For example, a physical region could be based on temperature.

_____

_____

_____

_____

2. Write the names of as many human regions as you can find. For example, a human region could be based on farming.

_____

_____

_____

_____

B. Choose any one of the physical or human regions from the article, map skills lesson, or this activity to read more about. Then complete the chart below. Write the name of your region in the space at the top. Show your region's location by outlining it on the map. List some features you think are characteristic of your region.

Region

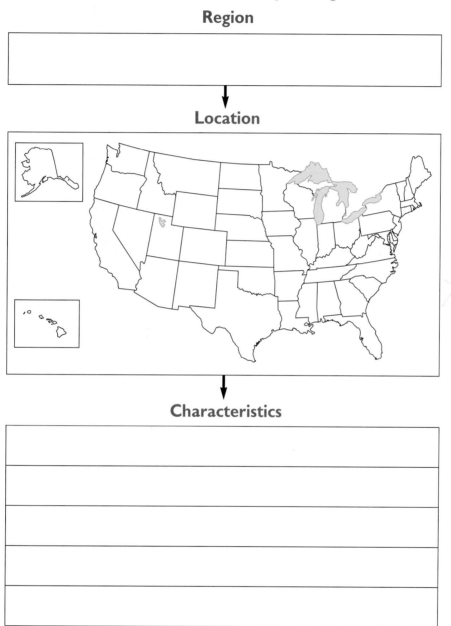

Location

Characteristics

C. Get together with a partner and describe your region aloud. Include characteristics of your region and similarities to other regions. Challenge your partner to identify it and tell whether the region is physical or human. Then compare your maps. How are they similar? How are they different? Do your regions overlap?

Lesson 3
Time Changes Things

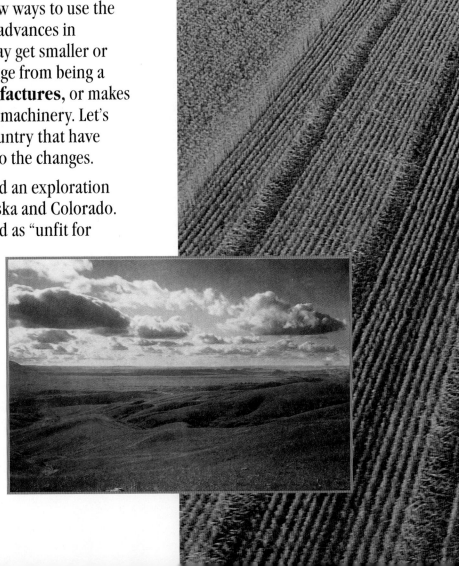

As you read about how the Great Plains and Great Lakes regions have changed, think about the role geography played in those changes.

Regions, like almost everything else, change with the passing of time. Think about yourself. Are you different today than you were a month ago, a year ago, or five years ago? How have you changed?

Regions change as people find new ways to use the land and its resources, or as new advances in technology are made. A region may get smaller or larger or break apart. It may change from being a farming region to one that **manufactures,** or makes a large number of products using machinery. Let's take a look at two areas of our country that have changed over time and what led to the changes.

In 1820 Major Stephen H. Long led an exploration party through present-day Nebraska and Colorado. He described the flat, treeless land as "unfit for cultivation, and of course uninhabitable by a people depending upon agriculture for their subsistence." Major Long named the area the "Great American Desert." This area included the present-day states of North Dakota, South Dakota, Nebraska, Kansas, Oklahoma, Montana, Wyoming, New Mexico, Colorado, and Texas within its boundaries.

Was the land uninhabitable? It may have been at first. But, because of advances in agriculture, such as the steel plow, the land indeed became inhabitable. This farming tool made it possible for people to till the land. Over time, further advances in farming tools were made, such as the tractor and combine. Now the part of the Great American Desert known as the Great Plains is one of the world's greatest wheat-producing regions. Another part of the Great American Desert, called the Sunbelt, is now home to many retired people. These retired people settle there because of the warm climate and attractive standard of living.

Other regions that have changed are the Northeast and Great Lakes regions. Manufacturing in North America began in the 1840s in southern New England. The rapid speed and large volume of goods being manufactured during this time led to an Industrial Revolution. During this period of high industry, the leading industrial states stretched from Massachusetts to Illinois.

Today manufacturing is still important to the Great Lakes region. Part of the Great Lakes area is sometimes called the "rust belt" because of the decline of some industries. Southern New England's current strength lies in its people's technical skills and in the region's educational institutions. Tourism is also an important source of income for the New England region. Thousands of visitors come each year to see its many historical sites.

Lesson 3
MAP SKILLS Using Maps to Learn About Changes in Regions

Maps can show recent or past information about places and people. We can compare maps from different time periods to see changes over time.

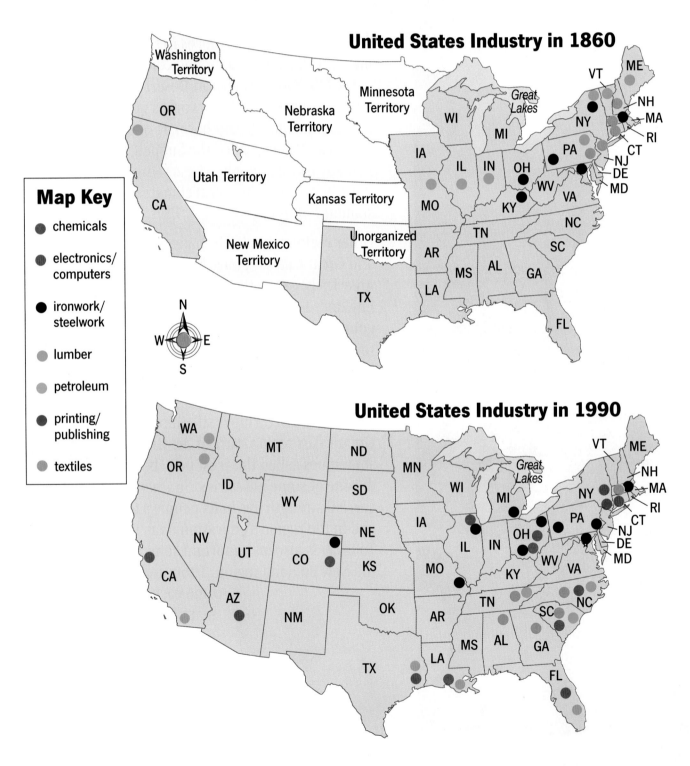

United States Industry in 1860

Washington Territory

OR

Minnesota Territory

Nebraska Territory

Map Key

- ● chemicals
- ● electronics/ computers
- ● ironwork/ steelwork
- ● lumber
- ● petroleum
- ● printing/ publishing
- ● textiles

CA

Utah Territory

Kansas Territory

New Mexico Territory

Unorganized Territory

N
W   E
S

VT   ME
NH
MA
RI
CT
NJ
DE
MD

Great Lakes

WI
MI
IA
IL   IN   OH
MO   KY   WV   VA
AR   TN   NC
MS   AL   GA   SC
LA
TX
FL

NY
PA

United States Industry in 1990

WA
MT   ND
OR
ID   WY
NV   UT   CO
CA   AZ   NM
MN
SD
NE
KS
OK
TX
WI
IA
MO
AR
LA
MI
IL   IN   OH
KY   WV   VA
TN   NC
MS   AL   GA   SC
FL
Great Lakes
VT   ME
NH
MA
RI
CT
NJ
DE
MD
NY
PA

16

A. Look at the map of United States industry in 1860. Answer the following questions.

   1. What were the states involved in industry?

_____

_____

_____

_____

   2. What were the main industries?

_____

_____

B. Compare the 1860 map with the 1990 map. Answer the following questions.

   1. Which states became industry centers in 1990 that were not in 1860?

_____

_____

_____

_____

   2. What types of industries have developed since 1860?

_____

_____

C. What do the maps show you about how regions of industry changed from 1860 to 1990?

_____

_____

_____

_____

Lesson 3

ACTIVITY
Find out the role geography plays in defining regions of the United States.

What A Place Makes

The **BIG**
Geographic Question

In what way does geography affect the types of industries that exist in regions of the United States?

From the article you learned how two regions of the United States changed over time. The map skills lesson showed you how to use two maps to evaluate changes in the industry of various regions. Now find out how a region's location affects the type of industry that exists there.

A. Look at the maps on page 16 again. List the different types of industry that were in each region in 1990.

1. Northeast and Great Lakes Region

a. _____

b. _____

c. _____

d. _____

2. Mid-Atlantic and Southeast Region

a. _____

b. _____

c. _____

d. _____

e. _____

3. West Coast Region

a. _____

b. _____

c. _____

B. Look at your lists above and answer the following questions.

1. Near what important physical feature are most of the states with industry located? _____

2. Is the physical feature you listed above an important resource needed to help make many of the goods you listed in Part A?

Why or why not? _____

_____

_____

_____

3. Write three of the listed industries that are most important to you.

_____   _____   _____

C. Select one of the industries listed above or one in the area where you live. Research how the industry you selected might be related to geography. Following are some questions to keep in mind while doing your research.

1. Where is the industry located?

2. What are the land, water, and resources (including people) in that location? Are they needed to make the product or good that this industry produces?

3. Was this industry important in the past? Is it important today? Why?

D. Make a one-page fact sheet about your selected industry to share with the class.

Lesson 4

LAND CHANGING HANDS

As you read about the history of the New England region, think about the many people who have lived in the area and their relationships to the land.

When the first Native Americans arrived in New England long ago, the land was good for growing a number of crops. They grew corn, blueberries, strawberries, beans, squash, grapes, tobacco, and Jerusalem artichokes.

Many years later, Giovanni da Verrazano, Samuel de Champlain, and John Smith were among the first Europeans to step upon and describe the New England coast. Verrazano,

an Italian captain exploring for France, described coastal land that was fertile and cultivated, except for the rocky coast of Maine. Champlain, also exploring for France, mapped and described some of the bays and harbors, especially Plymouth Harbor. English captain John Smith explored Boston Harbor and described the coast and islands as well populated and planted with fruit and corn.

Algonquian settle in Eastern Woodlands (New England)

Verrazano explores east coast

Champlain explores Plymouth Harbor

Smith explores Boston Harbor

Massachusetts Bay Colony settled

| 500s | 1500s | 1524 | 1605 | 1614 | 1620 | 1630 |

Iroquois form League of Five Nations

Pilgrims arrive at Plymouth Harbor

20

When the English settlers arrived on the Mayflower at Plymouth Harbor a few years later, they took over lands inhabited by Native Americans. The English were the first to establish settlements along the coast and inland in the river valleys. Shortly after their arrival, the English fought the French for control of North American lands in the French and Indian War. The English won all the French territory east of the Mississippi River, except for New Orleans.

As the English learned how to successfully farm the land, they grew crops such as corn and tobacco. Later they traded the crops with European buyers. Fishing also provided food for the colonists and income for exporters. The timber industry allowed the English to build wooden ships and houses and to trade lumber. The colonists found that the land provided many resources that were useful for survival.

When the English living in North America grew tired of the control that England had over them, they fought and defeated the British army in the Revolutionary War. A new nation was born. By the mid-1800s many European immigrants were coming to the United States to work in factories. As city populations grew and people had to be fed, farming took on new importance.

The feet of many different people have rested upon the land of New England over time. The land has changed many hands. Each of the different groups of people found ways to use the land that have left a lasting imprint.

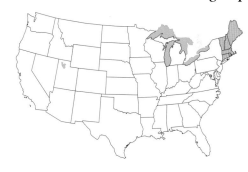

Continental Congress adopts Declaration of Independence

First Industrial Revolution

| 1775 | 1776 | 1788 | 1790 | 1791 | 1793 | 1848 |

American Revolution begins

Massachusetts, New Hampshire, and Connecticut become states

Rhode Island enters the Union

Vermont enters the Union

Big numbers of immigrants begin arriving from Europe

Lesson 4

MAP SKILLS Using a Map to Locate Natural and Human Features

Maps often show physical features, such as landforms and bodies of water. Maps can also show human features–exploration routes and places that people explored, settled, and named.

Early New England Region

Map Key

→ Verrazano (1524)

→ Champlain (1605)

→ Smith (1614)

▲ Mountains

🌲 Forests

— Present state boundaries

England
France

A. List the six states shown on the map that make up the New England region. Then label them on the map.

1. _____   4. _____

2. _____   5. _____

3. _____   6. _____

B. Use information from the article and Almanac to identify the following. After you identify these places, locate and label them on the map.

1. A name for the region of forests before European exploration

_____

Trace this region on the map.

2. The mountains of eastern North America that run through

New England _____
Draw these mountains on the map.

3. The ocean that the explorers crossed to get to North America _____
Label this ocean on the map.

4. The country that sent Giovanni da Verrazano and Samuel de Champlain

to explore coastal New England _____
Draw a line from this country to the New England region on the globe.

5. The country that sent John Smith to explore coastal New England _____
Draw a line from this country to the New England region on the globe.

6. The harbor that Champlain mapped and described _____
Label this harbor on the map.

7. The harbor that John Smith mapped and described _____
Label this harbor on the map.

Lesson 4
ACTIVITY
Find out how New Englanders have used their land over the years.

Using the Land

The **BIG** Geographic Question
How have different groups in history changed the land in New England?

From the article you learned about the people who settled the New England region. In the map skills lesson you identified the place where European explorers who came to the region landed. Now find out how people used New England's land long ago.

A. Using the chart below, show how each historical group used the land and what it looked like afterwards. Include in your answers what you know about these groups in terms of farming, manufacturing, and the timber industry.

Group of People	Time Period	Ways the Land Was Used	Effects on the Land
Native Americans			
First European Settlers			
Immigrants of the Industrial Revolution			

B. Looking at the information collected on your chart, how has land
use changed over time?

_____

_____

_____

_____

C. What does the New England region offer, in terms of its own
industries, that could benefit new businesses? Using the Almanac,
list the industries on the chart below. Then write how you think
each industry would benefit new businesses. (Possible answers include the following.)

Industry	Benefit

D. Imagine that you are at a meeting of New England governors.
You are to write a letter to businesspeople across the United States.
You are trying to get them to do business in the area. What would
you say to attract them? Write your letter on a separate piece of
paper and share it with the class.

Lesson 5

What's New in New England?

As you read about the New England region now, think about how its past geography compares to its geography today.

Sand dunes at Cape Cod, Massachusetts

Glaciers moving through New England some 12,000 years ago deposited rocks and boulders that made the soil thin and not very suitable for growing crops. These moving sheets of ice deposited ridges of sand that formed Cape Cod.

Native Americans in the New England area long ago found a way to cultivate the rocky land. New Englanders still plant, gather, and fish for foods in ways similar to those first cultivated by Native Americans. Lobster pots, or traps, are dropped in the coastal waters. Lobsters crawl into the pots to eat the bait. More lobsters are caught in Maine than in any other state.

Harbor scene in Maine

Buildings, another part of New England's past, still linger. Some of the oldest buildings in the United States are in this region. The Wayside Inn, on the old stagecoach road, in Sudbury, Massachusetts, opened in 1716. It is still open to the public for food and lodging. Elizabeth Portland Head Lighthouse, built in 1790, still warns ships away from the dangerous, rocky shores of Cape Elizabeth, Maine.

Wayside Inn today in Sudbury, Massachusetts

Meetinghouses often served as both a town hall and a place of worship in colonial days. All town meetings and elections were held there. Even today local government is often organized and managed through town meetings, at which every citizen can vote on any local law. In sharp contrast to the meetinghouses of the past are the skyscrapers of today. The 60-story John Hancock Tower can be found in Boston, Massachusetts, the largest city in New England.

New England is known for its autumn foliage. Tourists from many other states drive through the mountains to look at the beautiful red, orange, and gold leaves that have become a vivid image representing New England.

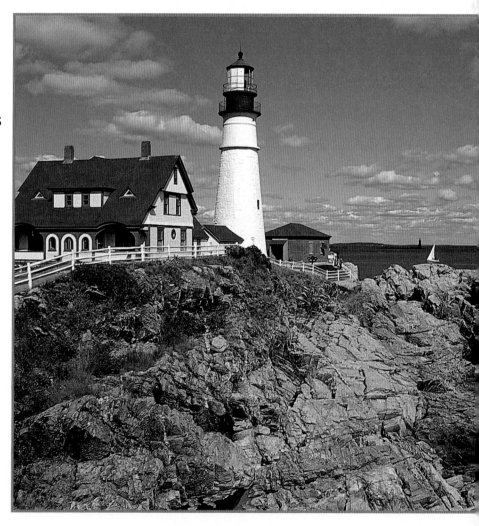

Elizabeth Portland Head Lighthouse in Cape Elizabeth, Maine

Lesson 5
MAP SKILLS Using Letters to Recall Map Elements

Acronyms are words formed by the first letters of a series of words. They are often used to help us remember a list of important things. The elements of a map are easy to recall with the help of an acronym.

New England Region, 1996
by SRA/McGraw-Hill

Legend

Mountains

Rivers

Lakes

★ State Capitals

CANADA

Mount Katahdin

ME

Penobscot River

Lake Champlain

Mount Washington

Augusta ★

Penobscot Bay

Montpelier ★

VT

A
P
P
A
L
A
C
H
I
A
N

M
O
U
N
T
A
I
N
S

NY

NH

★ Concord

Connecticut River

Atlantic Ocean

N
W E
S

★ Boston

MA

Cape Cod

Scale

0   100 Miles

0   100 Kilometers

Hartford ★

CT

★ Providence

RI

PA

Source: John Edwards and Associates

Index

Connecticut (CT) .... F2   New Hampshire (NH) G5
Maine (ME) .... I8   Rhode Island (RI) G2
Massachusetts (MA) .... F3   Vermont (VT) E6

A. Match each of the following words with one of the clues given below and reveal an acronym for map elements. The circled letters form the acronym.

Legend   Grid   Author   Date   Source
Title   Index   Orientation   Scale

1. Tells what the map is showing ◯ __ __ __ __

2. Tells what direction things appear in relation to each other

◯ __ __ __ __ __ __ __ __ __ __

3. Tells when the data was gathered ◯ __ __ __

4. Tells who gathered the data ◯ __ __ __ __ __

5. A box that shows the meanings of the symbols ◯ __ __ __ __ __

6. Used to compare map distance to actual distance ◯ __ __ __ __

7. Lists alphabetically the places shown on the map ◯ __ __ __ __

8. Helps find the location of a particular place on a map ◯ __ __ __

9. Shows who provided the data ◯ __ __ __ __ __

10. What is the acronym? __ __ __ __ __ __ __ __ __

B. Look at the New England regional map. Identify or describe the map elements using the acronym TODALSIGS.

1. T _____

2. O _____

3. D _____

4. A _____

5. L _____

6. S _____

7. I _____

8. G _____

9. S _____

Lesson 5

ACTIVITY
Make a map of the physical and human elements of the New England region.

A Map of New England

The **BIG** Geographic Question

What are some of the key physical and human elements of New England?

From the article you learned about physical and human features of New England. In the map skills lesson you learned an acronym to help you recall map elements. Now make a map showing physical and human elements of the New England region.

A. Look at the features listed on the chart below. Choose at least one of these New England resources to research in the Almanac. Take notes as you do your research.

Feature	What to Research	Almanac Notes
Mountains	name, where located	
Rivers	name, where located, mouth	
Vegetation	forest lands	
Natural Resources	types of natural resources	
Wildlife	types of wildlife	

B. Decide how you will show the information you have noted on a map. Use a sheet of scrap paper to plan and sketch your map. Then draw your map of the New England region in the space below. Give your map a title.

Lesson 6
FROM THE MOUNTAINS TO THE OCEAN

As you read about the coastal plains and mountain areas of the five Middle Atlantic states, think about how the physical features of an area affect what people do.

Visit a Pennsylvania Farm!

The Middle Atlantic region is one of great **diversity,** or many differences. Its five states—New York, New Jersey, Pennsylvania, Delaware, and Maryland—offer many choices of scenery and activities.

All of the Middle Atlantic states, except Pennsylvania, border the Atlantic Ocean. This gives them a seashore, which is great for swimming and even better for commercial fishing. The flat stretch of land along the shore is a **coastal plain.** Although Pennsylvania does not border the Atlantic Ocean, it does have a coastal plain. In fact, Philadelphia, Pennsylvania, is a major shipping port because it's just a short float down the Delaware River through the Delaware Bay off the Atlantic Ocean.

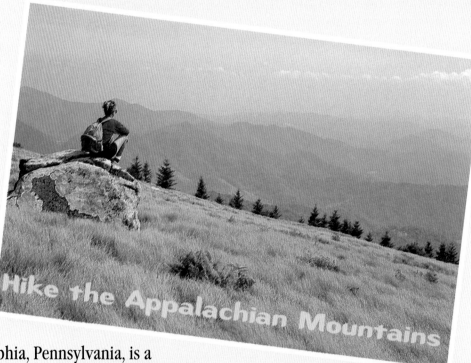

Hike the Appalachian Mountains

Water dominates the eastern shores of the Middle Atlantic, but go west and you'll find mountains–lots of them! The Appalachian Mountains await you. These scenic mountains have dramatic elevations that made traveling and trading difficult for early settlers in the United States.

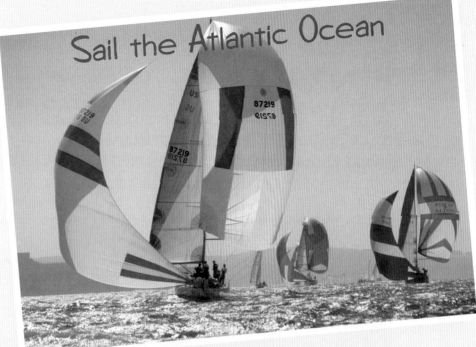

In 1817 American engineers began building the 363-mile Erie Canal to connect the Great Lakes with the Hudson River. Eight years later, the canal was completed and was the longest uninterrupted canal in the world. The Erie Canal provided quicker and easier travel and trade to the new states beyond the Appalachian Mountains.

Today highways and railroads connect the mountains with the seashore and people with the eastern and western cities. So whether you would like to hike the Blue Ridge Mountains or sail on the Atlantic Ocean, the Middle Atlantic region has just the place for you.

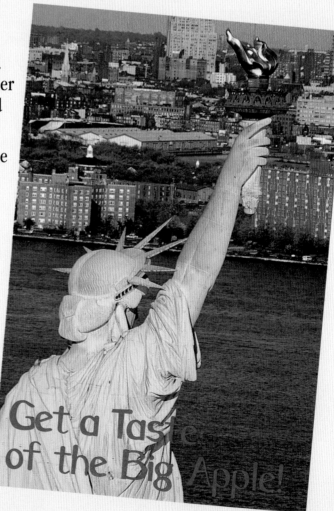

Lesson 6
MAP SKILLS Using an Elevation Key

We know that the land that a map shows us is not always flat.
We use a map's **elevation key** to help us understand the
shape of the land. **Elevation**, or **relief**, is measured in meters
or feet. It is the height the land rises above sea level.

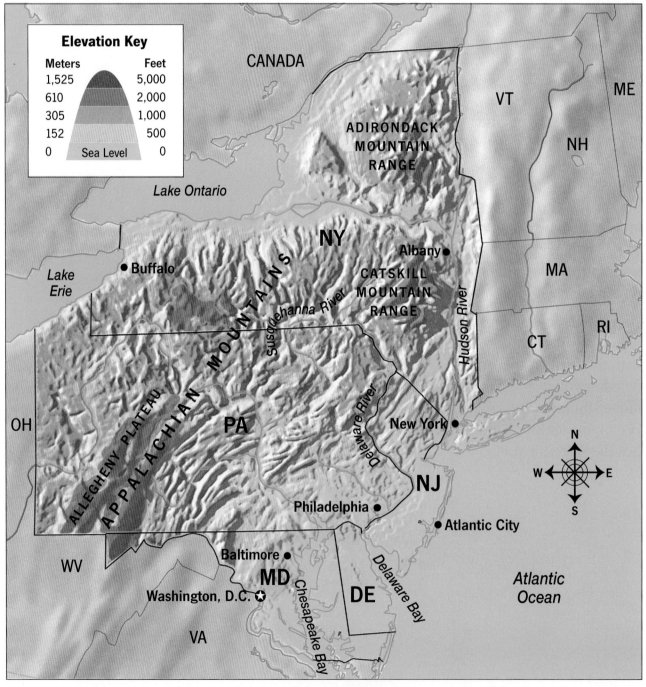

Elevation Key

Meters		Feet
1,525		5,000
610		2,000
305		1,000
152		500
0	Sea Level	0

CANADA

VT

ME

NH

ADIRONDACK
MOUNTAIN
RANGE

Lake Ontario

NY

Albany

MA

Buffalo

CATSKILL
MOUNTAIN
RANGE

Lake
Erie

M O U N T A I N S

Susquehanna River

Hudson River

RI

CT

OH

ALLEGHENY PLATEAU

A P P A L A C H I A N

PA

Delaware River

New York

N

NJ

W E

Philadelphia

Atlantic City

S

WV

Baltimore

MD

DE

Delaware Bay

Atlantic
Ocean

Washington, D.C. ✪

Chesapeake Bay

VA

A. Look at the elevation key to answer the following questions.

1. Write the elevation of the land shown in yellow.

   _____ meters   _____ feet

2. Which elevation is higher, the light green area or the orange area?

   _____

B. Look at the map of the Middle Atlantic region.

1. What is the elevation of most of the land along the Atlantic Ocean?

   _____

2. Describe how the land changes as you travel from west to east.

   _____

   _____

C. Find Buffalo, New York, on Lake Erie. Draw a line from west to east going from Buffalo to Albany, New York.

1. What two colors do you pass through? What are the elevations?

   a. Elevation color   **b.** Elevation in feet

   _____   _____

   _____   _____

2. What is the name of the mountain range north of the line that you drew?

   _____

3. Continue your line from Albany, New York, by tracing the Hudson River south

   to New York City. What is the elevation in feet? _____

4. Do you think the route from Buffalo to Albany was a good route for the

   Erie Canal? Why? _____

   _____

   _____

   _____

Lesson 6

ACTIVITY
Find out how the geography of a region influences where people live.

Why Live There?

> The **BIG** Geographic Question
>
> **How do the land and water of a region affect settlement patterns?**

In the article you read about the diverse physical features of the Middle Atlantic region. In the map skills lesson you looked at the elevation of this region. Now find out more about how geography affects people's locations and occupations.

A. Look in the Almanac for the population density map for the five states of the Middle Atlantic region.

1. Where is the population the greatest? Why?

_____

2. Which two states have the greatest rural areas?

_____   _____

3. What ocean is to the east of this region? _____

4. What two Great Lakes border the western side of this region?

_____   _____

5. List three major rivers in this region.

_____   _____   _____

6. List two big bays on the east coast.

_____   _____

7. List mountains in this region.

_____

B. Think about the geography and the population of the Middle Atlantic region.

    1. What do you notice about the relationship between the features of the land and where people live? _____

_____

_____

_____

    2. How do you think people decide where to live? _____

_____

_____

_____

_____

C. Now, using clay or papier-mâché, make a model of what you have learned about the Middle Atlantic region. Be sure to include the major landforms and waterways and mark the cities.

Here are a few hints:

- Glue yarn or string to your model to mark the major waterways.

- Use extra clay or papier-mâché to build up the mountain areas.

- Use flags made of toothpicks and small pieces of paper to mark the mountain ranges. Write the elevations on your flags.

- Make your own map key and symbols to show information. See an example below.

Sample Map Key
★ state capital
⬭ ocean
▲ mountains

Lesson 7

BosWash MEGA What?

As you read about the BosWash Megalopolis, think about how its geography makes it a different kind of region.

BosWash Megalopolis is the name given to the urban region that stretches along the Atlantic Ocean from north of Boston to south of Washington, D.C. It contains five major urban regions along the Middle Atlantic and southern New England coast—Boston, New York City, Philadelphia, Baltimore, and Washington, D.C.

Megalopolis comes from Greek words—*megas* means "great" and *polis* means "city." A megalopolis contains a number of cities and other urban areas where boundaries overlap. Its population density is so great that it appears to be one big city. At the center of the BosWash Megalopolis is New York City.

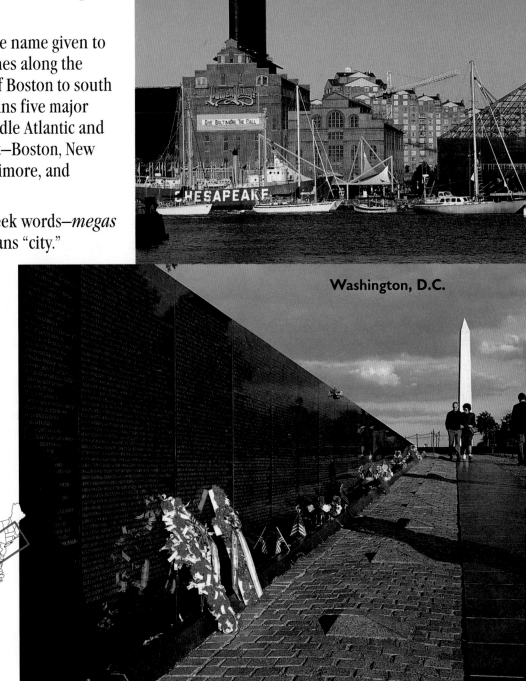

Baltimore

Washington, D.C.

The **BosWash Megalopolis** is a region of striking contrasts.

 It has rural areas that provide the cities with farm products and recreation.

 It has people from many different cultures.

 It is an area of great wealth and great poverty.

 It has fine museums and symphonies, but also areas with high crime rates.

 It has harbors, islands, sky-scrapers, and factories.

Boston

New York City

Philadelphia

The location of the BosWash Megalopolis is on the Atlantic Ocean, a busy ocean route between the United States and Western Europe. Most cars, ships, trains, and airplanes arrive and leave the United States at this "great city." Within this megalopolis you have some of the world's greatest harbors and ports, shores and coasts, population densities and diversity, and industry and trade all rolled into one great area.

39

Lesson 7

MAP SKILLS
Using Maps to Understand the BosWash Megalopolis

We can use a series of maps to see where a place is located within a larger area. The first map below shows New York City, one of the urban areas located in the BosWash Megalopolis. The second map shows where the BosWash Megalopolis is located in the larger New England and Mid-Atlantic regions. The third one shows where these regions are located in the United States.

Map 2

Map 1

Map 3

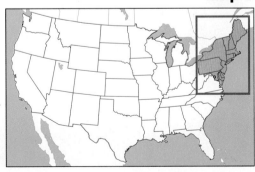

1. What is the name of the closest major city southwest of New York City? _____

_____

Which map showed you New York City with other major cities? _____

2. What building is located slightly southwest of the New York Public Library?

_____

Which map shows the building? _____

3. In what region is the state of New York located? _____

Which maps show you the state of New York in a region? _____

4. What street runs along the west side of Central Park? _____

Which map shows the street? _____

5. Look at the three maps and answer the following questions.

a. What river borders the east side of Manhattan? _____

b. What river borders the west side of Manhattan? _____

c. Which one of these rivers has two tunnels connecting New York and

New Jersey? _____

d. Name three boroughs, or sections, within New York City that are
shown on the map.

_____

_____

_____

6. Put an *X* in the box next to the map that shows a larger part of the United States.

[ ] Map 1   [ ] Map 2   [ ] Map 3

Lesson 7

ACTIVITY

Compare and contrast the five major urban regions of the BosWash Megalopolis.

Megalopolis Mania

The **BIG** Geographic Question

How are the urban regions of the BosWash Megalopolis alike and different?

From the article you learned what the BosWash Megalopolis is. The map skills lesson showed you New York City and the megalopolis on different scale maps. Now compare and contrast the five major urban areas that make up the BosWash Megalopolis.

A. On the chart below, write down some things you know about each urban area of the BosWash Megalopolis. Use the article and map skills lesson to help you with this information. One urban area has been done for you.

Megalopolis Urban Area	Where It's Located	Physical Features
Washington, D.C.	between Virginia and Maryland	• near Potomac River

B. Using the Almanac information, complete the following to learn how the megalopolis urban areas are alike and connected.

1. All five urban areas have populations

_____ under 500,000 _____ over 500,000.

2. All five urban areas have _____ airports that connect

them with each other and cities around the _____ .

3. All five urban areas are located near waterways, such as the

_____ Ocean or a _____ .

C. Use the information from your chart and the Almanac to create a 2- or 3-dimensional cityscape of the BosWash Megalopolis. A cityscape is a representation of a city's landscape. Plan your cityscape on a scrap piece of paper. Include all five urban areas and show that they are connected to form one region. Here are some suggestions.

- Draw and color or paint different kinds of landscapes on posterboard to represent each urban area's scenery. The scenery might include highways, railways, airports, seaports, and so on.

- Use index cards to draw and cut out the faces of features such as buildings, trees, or airplanes.

- Prop up all of your features by taping one end of a piece of cardboard against their back sides and the other end to the landscape.

- Write a description of the BosWash Megalopolis. Include information about each urban area's physical features and the transportation routes that connect them.

_____

_____

_____

_____

_____

_____

Lesson 8

Shrinking Swamps!

As you read about the fragile and unique swamps of southern Florida, think about the effects humans have had on these wetlands environments.

The Everglades in southern Florida is an area known as a "River of Grass." It has this nickname because the ground is always covered with a sheet of shallow water and grasses, shrubs, and trees. The shallow layer of water makes the area a **wetlands** region. Wetlands are areas, such as swamps and marshes, that have wet soils. The Big Cypress Swamp is another wetlands environment in southern Florida. It, too, is a low-lying wetland area with plant life poking through. **Watershed** is a feature common to these areas. It is all the water that eventually drains from a land area into a creek, lake, or river.

The Everglades and the Big Cypress Swamp are very fragile areas. This means they can easily be destroyed. The Everglades **ecosystem**—the plants and animals such as alligators, manatees, and the Florida panther that live in the area—is highly dependent on the water that flows through southern Florida. The Big Cypress Swamp shelters snakes, fish, and birds and plants such as cypress trees.

People did not always protect these fragile wetlands environments. For a long time, some people saw these wetland areas as wasteland ready to be used or developed. Other people saw them as places to drive off-road vehicles, which killed vegetation growing there. Some people chopped down the trees in these areas and did not plant new ones. Still other people collected plants and hunted the animals, disrupting the food chains.

When people started to see the abundance of life sustained by the Everglades, instead of preserving it they began draining the water to prepare it for farming. The land was cleared to plant sugarcane. People also built canals that connected Lake Okeechobee to the ocean. Eventually, the land was cleared enough to build cities and roads.

Each change damaged the area. There was a decline in wildlife. Plants and animals, such as numerous varieties of the colorful Florida tree snails, became extinct. Canals and cities changed the water flow and pushed back the boundaries of the swamps. People also brought pollution to the swamps.

Eventually, people began to realize the importance of the wetlands and the effects of their actions. Efforts are now being made to save the wetlands of Florida. The Big Cypress National Preserve and Everglades National Park were created to protect these areas. In addition, groups such as the Nature Conservancy are working hard to keep the lush marsh areas from shrinking even more!

The coastal wetlands in Southern Florida are among the most fragile environments in the United States. They are among the most important environments in Florida because they help control flooding, provide clean water, shelter wildlife, and support food chains. The changes that have occurred in these areas are examples of how human actions can modify physical environments. As people learn more about the abundance of life in these coastal wetlands, they can modify their actions to save these environments.

Lesson 8

MAP SKILLS
Using Maps to Compare Natural and Human-Made Features

Maps are created to show specific information such as roads, state borders, or physical features of the land. They can help us identify which physical features of the land are natural or human-made. These two kinds of physical features can be shown and compared on two maps.

Map A

Map B

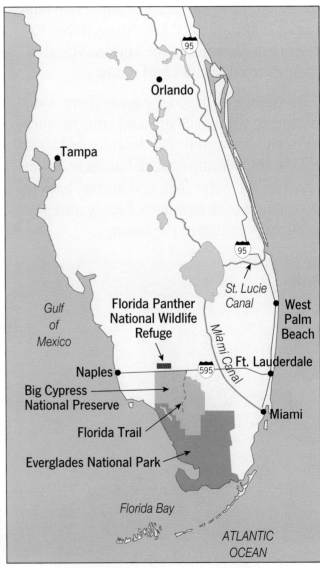

A. Look at the maps of southern Florida. Put an *X* on the following places on each map.

Map A
1. Lake Okeechobee
2. Big Cypress Swamp
3. Everglades
4. Kissimmee River

Map B
5. Florida Panther National Wildlife Refuge
6. Everglades National Park
7. Big Cypress National Preserve
8. Florida Trail

B. Use both maps to complete the following.

1. Indicate on which map you can find each of the following and whether each is natural or human-made.

   a. Big Cypress Swamp? _____

   b. Orlando? _____

   c. Big Cypress National Preserve? _____

   d. an interstate highway? _____

   e. a canal? _____

   f. rivers? _____

2. Look at Map B. Where are most of the cities located?

   _____

   _____

3. Draw the information from Map B onto Map A.
   a. Place the cities, roads, and canals on Map A.
   b. Add the boundaries to show Big Cypress National Preserve and Everglades National Park.
   c. Are any human-made features such as cities located inside Big Cypress

   National Preserve and Everglades National Park? _____

4. Now look at Map A. Describe how much of the Everglades and Big Cypress Swamp has been preserved by humans and what has happened to the remainder of the wetlands.

   _____

   _____

Lesson 8

ACTIVITY
Find out the pros and cons of changing fragile wetlands.

Changing Environments

The **BIG** Geographic Question

Should people develop or preserve fragile ecosystems like the wetlands in southern Florida?

From the article you learned that the wetlands of southern Florida are very fragile but important environments. In the map skills lesson you looked at some human-made versus natural features in southern Florida. Now find out what different groups want to do about the future of the wetlands.

A. Indicate what you know about the following wetland features. Add other features from the article or your own research. Write *N* for natural, *H* for human-made, + for positive impact on the wetlands, and − for negative impact on the wetlands.

Features	Type	Impact
parking lots		
paved roads		
cypress trees		
sawgrass		
canals		
alligator holes		

B. Imagine you have to present the viewpoint of a group that has a special interest in the wetlands of southern Florida. Choose one of the groups below. You might want to talk with an adult friend or family member to see what they know about the groups listed. Best of all, if you know someone who fits one of these descriptions, you might want to ask that person the questions in section **C** below. Circle the group whose ideas you want to represent.

1. Land developers—want to build new condominium complexes or vacation areas
2. Environmentalists—want to preserve the environment
3. City dwellers moving out of the city—want to move to a quiet place to enjoy nature and get away from the crowded city
4. Farmers—want land to farm and water to irrigate crops
5. Senior citizens retiring to southern Florida—want to move to a place with warm weather and plenty of recreational activities close to home

C. See how many of the following questions you can answer about your group. Do research if you need more information.

1. Does your interest group want to preserve or develop the wetlands?

_____

2. What has happened to the wetlands in the past that you think is good?

_____

3. What has happened to the wetlands in the past that you think is bad?

_____

4. What are your group's plans for the wetlands?

_____

5. Why would following your group's plans be a good idea?

_____

D. Present to a friend or family member your group's ideas on the issue of preserving versus changing the wetlands. Use books, pictures, and maps to enhance your presentation.

Lesson 9

From Cotton Belt to Sun Belt

As you read about the South, notice how geographical changes are bringing about a new look for the "Old South."

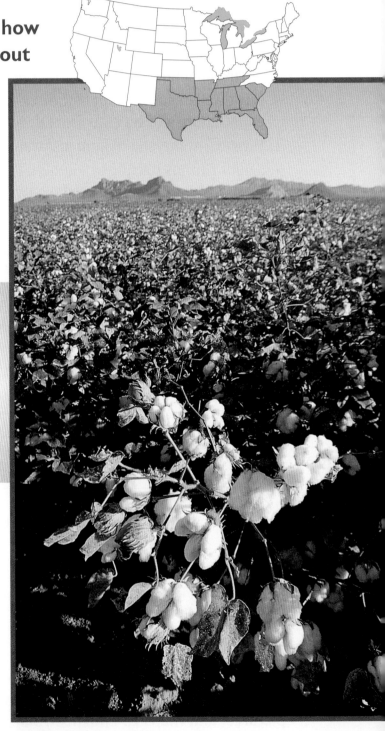

In the 1800s the South was known as the "Cotton Belt" because cotton was the main crop. Plantation owners put their money into growing cotton, and their profit came from selling it. Whether rich or poor, a free person or a slave, the lives of people in the South depended on cotton. In the "Old South," cotton was king.

Growing cotton did not always go smoothly. Some years plantation owners ruined their soil by growing only cotton. Then they had to buy more land. Other years plantation owners grew too much cotton, and the price of cotton was down. During these years, profits were low. Still other years the Mexican boll weevil destroyed the cotton. Then the plantation owners made no money.

In the 1860s the Civil War brought change to the "Old South." Before the Civil War, plantation owners had slaves to plant and harvest the cotton. After the Civil War, plantation owners could no longer own slaves. They needed lots of workers, but they had no money to pay the workers. Many large plantations were divided into small farms. Freed African American slaves became tenant farmers, paying rent to farm on land that had once been part of their former owner's large plantation.

A field of cotton in Mississippi

By the 1900s people were moving from farms to the cities. People in the cities needed jobs. In the 1930s the Tennessee Valley Authority (TVA) built dams along the rivers that helped provide electricity needed by factories in the region. Between 1900 and 1940 14 million people left farms in the South, including about two million African Americans. The attraction of jobs in factories encouraged many people to move to the Midwest, Northeast, and California. Poor conditions in the South also gave many a reason to leave.

This Tennessee dam produces electricity used by businesses.

Eventually, better ways of communicating and better roads brought businesses to the South. State and local governments offered tax breaks to industries that moved into the area. Between 1940 and 1980 industry in the South doubled, and cities grew. The people who lived in the South could now find jobs in occupations such as food processing, textiles, and the military. The "Old South" was changing, and a "New South" was taking shape.

The South's warm climate began to attract more and more people. The invention of air-conditioning made it possible to work comfortably in large buildings year-round. Some people moved south to retire. Others went to enjoy the warm weather and visit the many beaches and historical sites.

Tourism eventually became one of the big industries of the South. In fact, Atlanta, Georgia, was home to the 1996 Summer Olympics. This event presented the image that the South wants the world to see—a "New South" that is modern, broad-minded, and linked to the world. Today the cotton belt of the "Old South" prefers to be known as the sunbelt of the "New South."

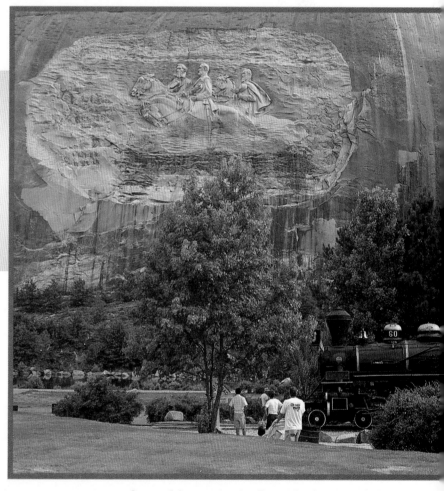

Stone Mountain, in Georgia, is one of the South's many historic sites.

51

Lesson 9
MAP SKILLS
Using Maps to Study Industry Location Change Over Time

Map A shows where centers of industry were located before the Civil War in the 1860s. Map B shows where centers of industry were located in 1990. We can use these maps to figure out how industrial locations have changed over time.

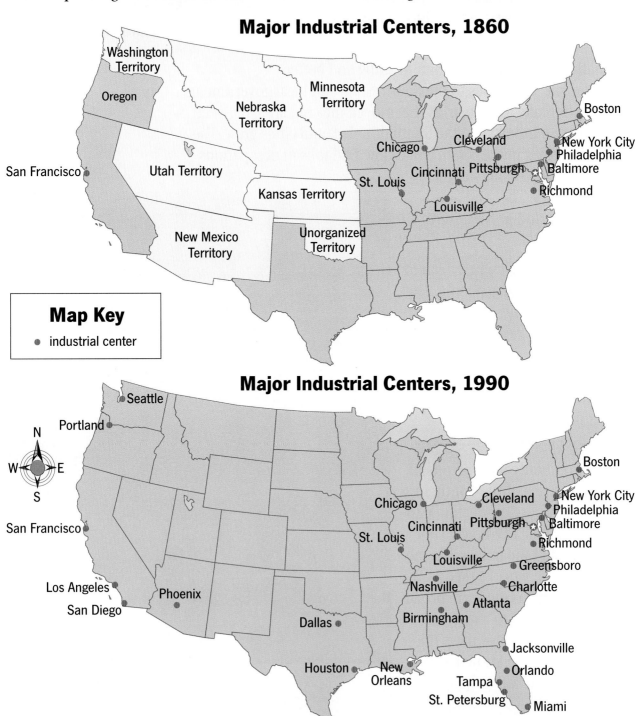

Major Industrial Centers, 1860

Washington Territory

Oregon

Minnesota Territory

Nebraska Territory

Boston

San Francisco

Utah Territory

Chicago
Cleveland
New York City
Philadelphia
Cincinnati
Pittsburgh
Baltimore

St. Louis

Kansas Territory

Richmond

Louisville

New Mexico Territory

Unorganized Territory

Map Key
- industrial center

Major Industrial Centers, 1990

Seattle

Portland

N
W   E
S

Chicago
Cleveland
New York City
Philadelphia
Cincinnati
Pittsburgh
Baltimore

Boston

San Francisco

St. Louis

Richmond

Louisville
Greensboro

Los Angeles

Phoenix

Nashville
Charlotte

San Diego

Atlanta

Dallas

Birmingham

Jacksonville

Houston

New Orleans

Orlando

Tampa

St. Petersburg
Miami

A. Look at the maps and answer the following questions.

1. In 1860, were most of the cities located in the northeastern states or the southeastern states? _____

2. In 1990, where were most of the cities located? _____

_____

3. What cities were important industrial centers in 1990 that were not important in 1860? _____

_____

_____

4. To what areas did industry spread in 1990? _____

_____

B. Looking at the maps and your answers to the above questions, draw some conclusions about how the location of major industrial centers has changed over time.

1. Read the statement: Manufacturing moved from the industrial northeast to the "New South." Explain why you agree or disagree with this statement.

_____

_____

_____

_____

2. Why do you think most of the industrial centers in 1860 and 1990 were mainly on the east and west coasts?

_____

_____

_____

_____

Lesson 9

ACTIVITY Find out what makes a good tourist attraction.

"Hot" Tourist Spots

The **BIG** Geographic Question

Why has tourism become such big business in the Southeast?

From the article you learned about the South and how it has changed. The map skills lesson showed you how the location of industrial centers changed over time. Now find out why tourism has become such a big business in the Southeast.

A. Circle one of the following tourist attractions in the Southeast, or write the name of another southeast destination that you would like to know more about.

- Civil Rights Monument
- Kennedy Space Center
- The Appalachian Trail

- Walt Disney World
- Smoky Mountain National Park
- The Everglades National Park

B. Answer as many of the following questions as you can about the tourist attraction you selected. Use a pencil so you can change your answers later by checking them against the Almanac information.

1. Where is your tourist destination located? _____

2. What is the climate like there? _____

3. What are some specific things to do there? _____

   _____

4. What else is nearby that is of interest? _____

   _____

5. How could you travel there? _____

C. What do you think are important features of a tourist attraction or destination? Use the chart below to indicate your rating by marking a + if the feature is important. Mark a − if the feature is not important. Then ask two classmates or family members for their ratings.

Feature of Tourist Attraction	Your Rating	Person 1 Rating	Person 2 Rating
places to camp nearby			
places to eat nearby			
cost to get in			
location			
weather and climate			
other tourist sites nearby			
educational			
fun			
variety of activities			
shopping			

D. Design a travel brochure for that tourist attraction. Include pictures, a map, or any other graphic that will add interest to your brochure. The brochure should include reasons why people should visit the site. Use ideas from the chart above. Then look over your travel brochure and those of your classmates. What common feature is important in attracting people to the Southeast?

_____

_____

_____

_____

HEARTLAND, USA!

As you read about the Midwest region, think about how its geography makes it the "Heartland."

The Midwest includes 12 states that are located in the center of the United States. This is one reason this region is often called the "Heartland" of the country. Another reason is that some people think that Midwesterners still live like early settlers of the United States did—farming the land, living in small towns, and leading a slower paced lifestyle. Many Midwesterners share this view of their region, even though the Midwest has large cities like Chicago, Illinois, and St. Louis, Missouri.

Part of the Midwest region was once covered with wild prairie grass. Now it is covered with grains. The area has rich soil, a good climate for farming, and in most areas, a plentiful supply of water. This makes it an excellent place for growing crops such as corn or raising livestock such as cows. The Corn Belt, the Wheat Belt, and the Dairy Belt are all in the Midwest.

The Midwest is also known as the "industrial heartland" of America. Many major midwestern cities became famous in the 1950s and 1960s for their manufactured products. Detroit, Michigan, has traditionally been known for its automobile industry. Gary, Indiana, has been known for its steel mills. Chicago, Illinois, has been known for its meat-packing industry. Minneapolis, Minnesota, has been known for its flour mills. These products have been transported all over the world by way of the country roads, interstate highways, railroads, rivers, and lakes of the Midwest.

The Midwest has huge cities such as Chicago.

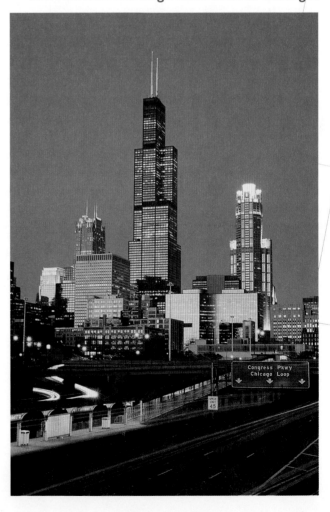

What do you see when you travel around the Midwest today? You see big cities and small towns. You see grain and dairy farms, as well as factories. There are farmers' markets and grocery superstores. You travel interstate highways and gravel roads. You see small airfields and major airports. You meet people from a variety of ethnic backgrounds. You see what many people think of as "typical" Americans—farmers, factory workers, business people, educators, and truck drivers. You see all the reasons the Midwest is called the "heartland" of the United States.

The Midwest has miles of farmland, like these broad, flat plains in Kansas.

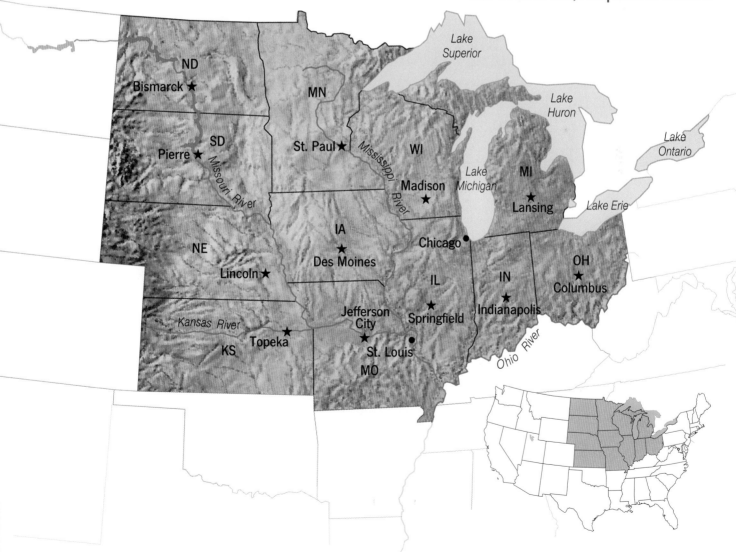

Lesson 10

MAP SKILLS
Using a Dot Map to Identify Grain Belts of the Midwest

Maps can show where crops are grown. Maps can also show how much of an area is planted with different crops. Knowing where a crop is grown and how much of it is grown in an area helps you identify the "belt," or zone, for that crop. Some areas of the Midwest are known as the Corn Belt, the Winter Wheat Belt, and the Spring Wheat Belt.

Corn and Wheat Belts

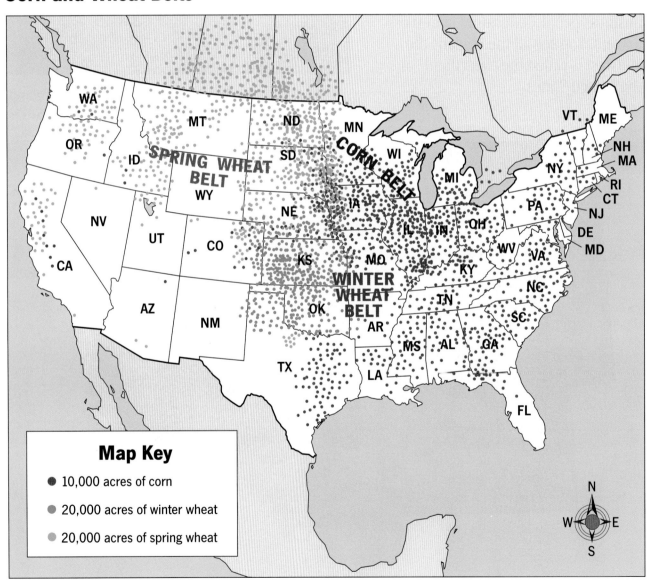

Map Key
- 10,000 acres of corn
- 20,000 acres of winter wheat
- 20,000 acres of spring wheat

A. Look at the map and circle the following.
1. Illinois
3. Nebraska
5. Missouri
2. Iowa
4. Arizona
6. Map key

B. Use the map and map key to answer the following questions.

1. **a.** What does a red dot mean? _____

   b. What does a green dot mean? _____

2. **a.** Name at least five states where corn is grown. _____

   _____

   _____

   b. How do you know corn is grown in the states you named? _____

   _____

C. Answer the following.

1. How many dots do you see in Arizona? _____

2. What color is each dot? _____

   _____

3. How many acres of corn are grown in Arizona? _____

   How do you know? _____

4. Is more corn grown in Arizona or Illinois? _____

   Explain how you know. _____

   _____

D. Write a few sentences comparing the amount of corn grown in Ohio to the amount of corn grown in Missouri.

_____

_____

_____

_____

Lesson 10

ACTIVITY
Find out how a natural disaster affects people–directly and indirectly.

Floods, Farmers, and Food

The **BIG**
Geographic Question

How does a natural disaster in one region affect people in another region?

From the article you learned that the Midwest is known as the industrial and farming heartland of the United States. A dot map in the map skills lesson helped you locate corn and wheat belts in the Midwest. Now find out how something that happens in one region of the United States can touch the lives of people in another region and sometimes all over the world.

A. List some natural disasters that you think could hurt a farmer's crops.

1. _____   4. _____

2. _____   5. _____

3. _____   6. _____

B. The Great Midwestern Flood of 1993 was a natural disaster. Try to answer as many of the following questions as you can about the flood. Use a pencil so you can change your answers later. Look in the Almanac to check and adjust your answers.

1. List the nine states that were directly affected by the flood. _____

   _____

2. Which two rivers were the main source of the flood waters? _____

   _____

3. What were some of the crops grown in the flood area? _____

   _____

C. Many people felt the effects of the Great Flood of 1993. Read each effect. Mark *D* if it *directly* affected the people; mark *I* if it *indirectly* affected the people.

Effect	People in Flood Area	People Outside Flood Area
1. Flood waters and river bottom sand covered farm fields.		
2. Homes and other structures were filled with water and mud.		
3. Roads closed and bridges washed away.		
4. Drinking water was contaminated.		
5. Farmers couldn't harvest crops or plant new crops.		
6. Volunteers helped flood victims.		
7. Certain foods were in short supply in the grocery stores.		

D. Use the information from the article, the map skills lesson, the Almanac, and the information you collected above to create a news broadcast about the flood. Describe the areas directly affected by the Great Midwestern Flood of 1993. Describe the physical features involved and the problems caused by the flood. Write your broadcast below.

_____

_____

_____

_____

_____

Lesson 11

Dust Storm!

As you read about the causes of the Dust Bowl, think of how people used and changed the land in this region.

In the 1860s many Americans in the East wanted land to farm. The government wanted land in the Midwest and Great Plains to be settled. It offered free land in this region to people who would farm it. Thousands of settlers accepted the offer. A westward move was on!

Many settlers found farming on the Great Plains hard. The soil was fertile, but farther west, farmers could not depend on rainfall levels from year to year. This area was part of what Major Stephen Long had called the "Great American Desert." Farmers had to irrigate the land to water their crops. They pumped water from the ground using the power of the wind that swept over the plains.

Soon wheat and other grains grew where cattle used to graze. In fact, the farmers pushed the cattle ranchers farther west. Cattle overgrazed the thin grass of the western Great Plains, eating so much grass that it could not grow back. Large areas of soil were left bare to the wind.

Dust Bowl
Great Plains States

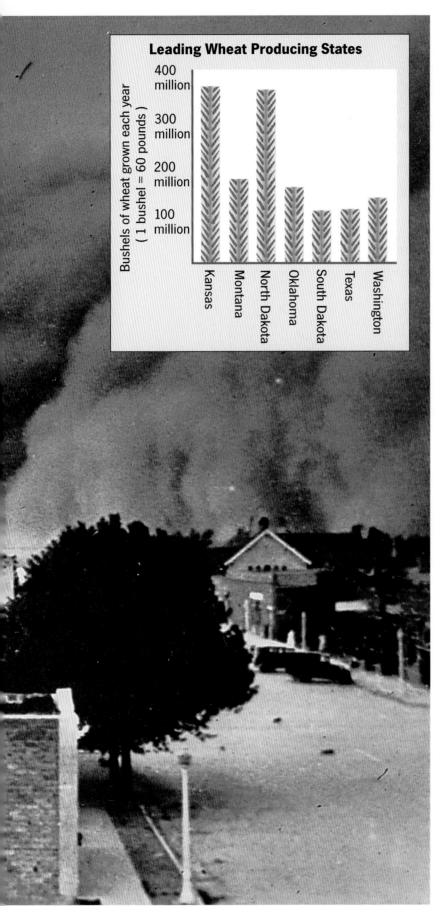

Leading Wheat Producing States

Bushels of wheat grown each year
(1 bushel = 60 pounds)

400 million
300 million
200 million
100 million

Kansas • Montana • North Dakota • Oklahoma • South Dakota • Texas • Washington

Then in the early 1900s, tractors and combines were invented. These new farm machines helped farmers plant even more land with wheat. But wheat did not hold the soil together against the wind the way grass roots had. When a long drought began in 1931, the soil dried up into fine, loose dust. And when the strong winds of the Great Plains began to blow, they picked up the dust and whirled it around.

One of the first huge dust storms carried tons of dirt from the Great Plains all the way to the East Coast! In cities like Chicago and Detroit the streetlights had to be turned on at noon because the blowing dust darkened the normally bright afternoon skies. Over the next four years of drought, dust storms swept across the plains. People and animals who were caught in the storms could barely breathe. Some became lost. Dust blew into homes so thickly that it had to be shoveled out. It buried cars and tractors, ruining them. Many people could not afford to keep their farms.

People tried to find solutions to help reduce the power of the wind. One of the solutions was to plant lines of trees to break the wind's force. Another solution included building wooden-slated wind fences. Farmers began using these methods to conserve, or protect, the soil from the wind. Dust storms still occur during dry periods on the plains, but soil conservation has reduced the negative effects.

The skies of the Great Plains were once blackened by mighty clouds of dust.

Lesson 11

MAP SKILLS

Using a Map to Find
Where a Crop Is Grown

The map below uses shades of color to represent the different wheat belts in North America. The northern wheat belt is the spring wheat belt. Wheat is planted in the spring and harvested in the fall. The southern wheat belt is the winter wheat belt. Wheat is planted in the fall and harvested in the spring.

Wheat-Producing Areas of North America

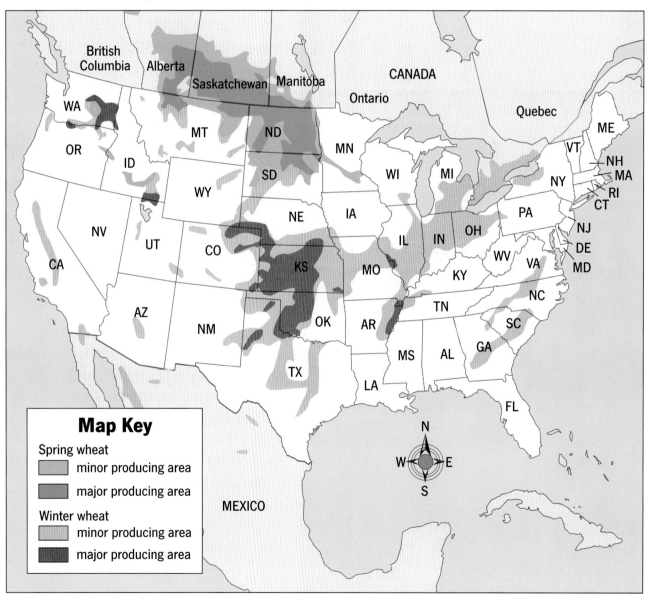

Map Key

Spring wheat
- minor producing area
- major producing area

Winter wheat
- minor producing area
- major producing area

A. Look at the map and complete the following.

1. Underline the names of the states in the northern spring wheat belt.

2. Circle the names of the states in the southern winter wheat belt.

B. Answer the following questions about where the different kinds of wheat are grown.

1. Which two states grow the most wheat? _____

_____

2. Which states produce both spring and winter wheat? _____

_____

_____

3. Which states are minor producers of winter wheat? _____

_____

_____

_____

4. Is there more winter wheat or spring wheat grown in the United States? _____

_____

5. Which three spring wheat producing states grow the smallest amount of spring wheat?

_____

_____

6. Where in North America is the most spring wheat grown?

_____

_____

Lesson 11

ACTIVITY
Find out about crops that are grown on the plains and how they are used.

Growing Grains

The BIG Geographic Question

What agricultural products do we get from the Midwestern plains?

In the article you read about how people started growing wheat on the plains and what effect it had on the land. The map skills lesson showed where wheat is grown in the Midwest today. Now find out more about crops grown in the Midwest and the uses people have for them.

A. Use the Almanac to find where wheat, corn, and soybeans are grown in the Midwest. List the crops and the Midwestern plains states where each crop is grown.

Crop	Where Grown
Wheat	
Corn	
Soybeans	

B. Find out how each crop is used. First look through your home for products made from each crop. Then find out about other uses. Try to find at least four uses for each crop and list them below. At least two uses should be something other than food items.

_____

_____

_____

_____

66

C. On a separate sheet of paper, make a chart like the one below. List the crops you learned about. List the Midwestern states where they are grown, and picture or list some uses of each crop.

Crop	Where Grown	Uses
Wheat	North Dakota	bread

D. Choose one Midwestern plains crop. Write about how important this crop is in people's everyday lives. What might happen if flooding or storms destroyed much of this crop during a growing season?

_____

_____

_____

_____

_____

_____

_____

_____

_____

_____

_____

_____

Lesson 12
A Southwestern Scrapbook

As you read about the American Southwest of long ago, think about how different cultures used similar environments and the land's natural resources in different ways.

The southwestern region of the United States is like a scrapbook. Pictures of its people, cultures, and communities give us many clues about the land long ago. Each culture used the natural resources of Earth: stone, clay, and mud. Each culture, however, used the resources in very different ways.

Long before the United States became a nation, prehistoric people such as the Anasazi tribe made their homes in the Southwest. They were known as the "cliff dwellers" because they had a unique way of building shelters using Earth's resources. They built their homes and communities into the sides of steep hills and mountains. The Zuni Native American tribe built apartmentlike villages. These Native Americans became known as the Pueblos, the Spanish word for "town" or "village." The pueblo style of architecture is still used today. The buildings appear to grow out of the land; some even look like landforms.

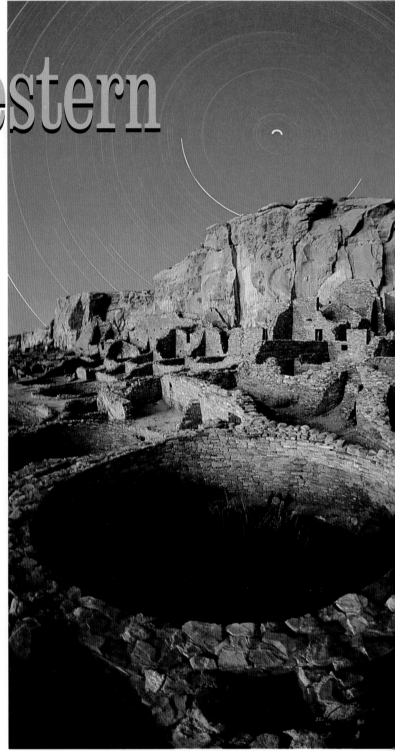

The largest early pueblo building was Pueblo Bonito in New Mexico, built between 900 and 1000 A.D. Pueblo Bonito has over 800 rooms.

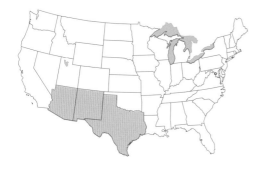

In the 1500s the Spanish established towns across the Southwest. Spanish towns built around a central plaza became part of the architecture of the Southwest. They used adobe—bricks made from clay, water, straw, and grass. The word *adobe* is the Spanish name for sun-dried bricks or a house built with these special bricks. Adobe homes and other buildings stayed cool in summer and warm in winter.

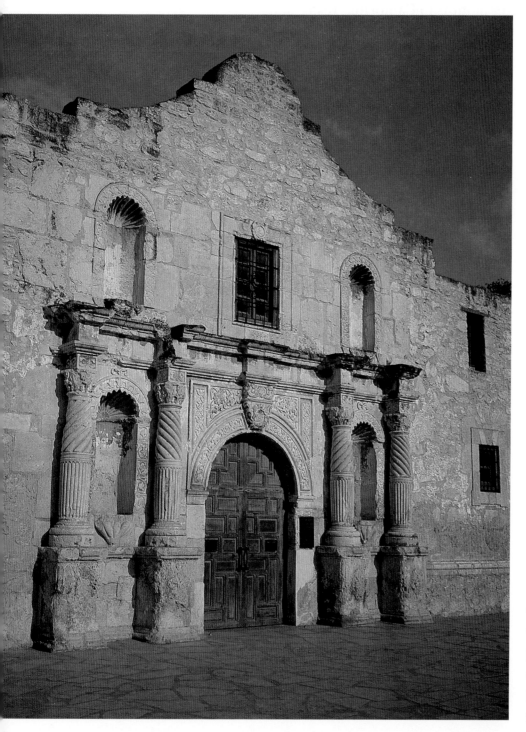

In the 1800s another group of people moved to the Southwest. These people came from northern Europe and the eastern part of the United States and included many Germans. They used yet another resource to build their homes, forts, and other buildings— limestone. Limestone is a strong rock that can be carved and cut without splitting.

People traveling in the Southwest today can find traces of all of these cultures. They can see cliff dwellings, adobe pueblos, and limestone structures. Each one is a reminder of the people who lived in the Southwest many years ago.

The Alamo in San Antonio, Texas, is built of limestone. It was built in 1718 as a Catholic Mission and was later used by Texans as a military fort.

Lesson 12

MAP SKILLS Using Maps to Understand Migration Patterns

Migration is the movement of people from one place to another. A population map shows the movement patterns in a specific region. It helps us to understand how and why people move and where they settle.

Migrant workers spend the winter months in California, Texas, and Florida. Then they move to work the harvest of crops farther north.

Major Routes of Migrant Workers in the United States

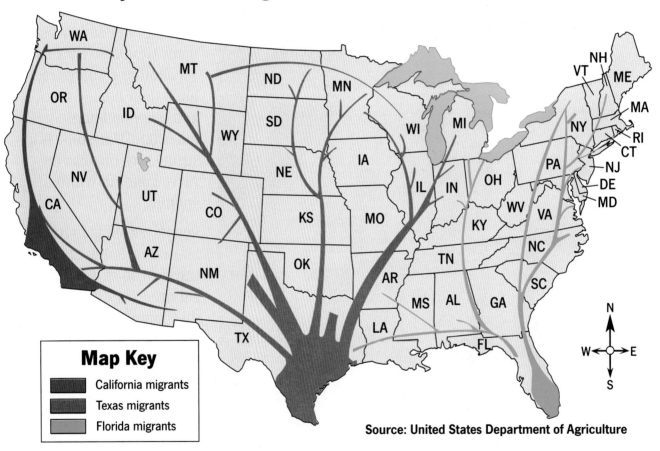

Map Key
- California migrants
- Texas migrants
- Florida migrants

Source: United States Department of Agriculture

A. Look at the migration map. Trace these three states on the map.

1. California (CA)

2. Texas (TX)

3. Florida (FL)

B. Use the map to complete the following.

1. What is the source of this migration map?

_____

2. Read the map's title. What do the three states represent on the map?

_____

_____

3. In which direction did the workers migrate?

_____

4. Why do you think the farm workers migrate to the north in the summer?

_____

_____

5. Suggest other reasons why people might move from one place to another.

_____

_____

6. Choose one migration route and circle it on your map. Describe how the route moves and changes. Be sure to use direction words (north, south, east, west) and the state names in your description.

_____

_____

_____

Lesson 12

ACTIVITY Create a cultural collage of the Southwest.

A Southwestern Collage

The BIG Geographic Question

Who are the people of the Southwest, and what are their customs?

From the article you learned about different cultures that lived in the Southwest long ago. The map skills lesson showed you how to use a map to understand movement patterns of migrant workers. Now make a collage of pictures and words about the cultures of the Southwest, past and present.

A. Write the names of the states in the southwestern region of the United States.

_____

_____

B. In the box below, draw a simple map of the Southwest. Label the states.

C. Use the article and the Almanac to find out more about the Southwest. As you learn about the region, take notes about the different people who live there and their cultures.

Characteristics of	Notes
People	
Food	
Language	
Clothing	
Customs	
Climate	
Land	
Water	
Buildings	

D. Look through magazines and newspapers. Cut out pictures or words that represent the southwestern cultures. You might want to draw pictures and write words of your own to add to your collection.

E. Put your drawings, pictures, and words together to make a large collage about the Southwest. Share your collage with the class.

Lesson 13

"A "GRAND" CANYON"

As you read about the Grand Canyon, think about the effects of water on the land.

Imagine you're walking along a high desert plateau in the southwestern United States. Suddenly the ground seems to fall away from under your feet. A huge, gaping hole stretches for miles before you. It's so deep and wide that you can't see its bottom. You've found a **gorge**—a deep, narrow opening between steep and rocky walls or sides of mountains.

At the bottom of the Grand Canyon is the force that created it—the waters of the Colorado River. Over millions of years, this river has scoured, gouged, and carried away the land around it. It has carved a **canyon**, a deep valley with steep sides, usually with a stream running through it. The canyon is two billion years old!

The beautifully colored layers of rock in the canyon walls are like a history book. Each rock layer tells what the land was like at a certain time in the past. It also contains fossils that tell about the plants and animals that lived during that time.

The Grand Canyon is one of the United States' most popular places to visit. People marvel at its vastness and peacefulness.

74

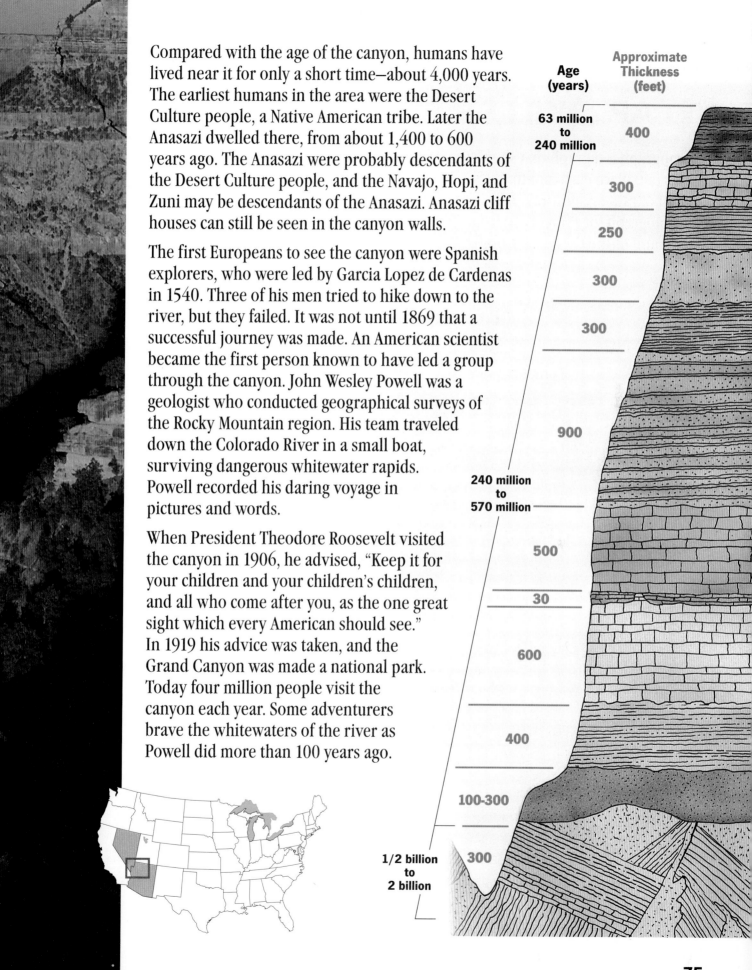

Compared with the age of the canyon, humans have lived near it for only a short time—about 4,000 years. The earliest humans in the area were the Desert Culture people, a Native American tribe. Later the Anasazi dwelled there, from about 1,400 to 600 years ago. The Anasazi were probably descendants of the Desert Culture people, and the Navajo, Hopi, and Zuni may be descendants of the Anasazi. Anasazi cliff houses can still be seen in the canyon walls.

The first Europeans to see the canyon were Spanish explorers, who were led by Garcia Lopez de Cardenas in 1540. Three of his men tried to hike down to the river, but they failed. It was not until 1869 that a successful journey was made. An American scientist became the first person known to have led a group through the canyon. John Wesley Powell was a geologist who conducted geographical surveys of the Rocky Mountain region. His team traveled down the Colorado River in a small boat, surviving dangerous whitewater rapids. Powell recorded his daring voyage in pictures and words.

When President Theodore Roosevelt visited the canyon in 1906, he advised, "Keep it for your children and your children's children, and all who come after you, as the one great sight which every American should see." In 1919 his advice was taken, and the Grand Canyon was made a national park. Today four million people visit the canyon each year. Some adventurers brave the whitewaters of the river as Powell did more than 100 years ago.

Age (years)

Approximate Thickness (feet)

63 million to 240 million

400

300

250

300

300

900

240 million to 570 million

500

30

600

400

100-300

1/2 billion to 2 billion

300

75

MAP SKILLS
Using a Climograph to Find Temperatures and Rainfall

A climograph is a graph that shows the average temperature at a certain place each month. It also shows the average amount of rain or snow that falls at the place monthly. Below is a climograph for Phoenix, Arizona. Phoenix lies about 200 miles south of the Grand Canyon.

Climograph of Phoenix, Arizona

KEY
temperature
rainfall

Average monthly temperature (Fahrenheit)

Rainfall in inches

JAN FEB MAR APR MAY JUNE JULY AUG SEPT OCT NOV DEC

A. Look at the climograph and complete the following.

1. Find and touch *January* at the bottom of the graph.

2. Move your finger up until you touch the colorful, horizontal line on the graph.

3. Move your finger to the left until you touch the column of numbers that stand for temperatures. The number nearest your finger is close to the average temperature in Phoenix in January. That temperature is about 52°F.

4. Down the right side of the graph, circle the number that stands for inches of rainfall.

B. The bars on the graph show inches of rainfall in Phoenix. To find the average rainfall in Phoenix in January, follow these steps.

1. Find and touch *January* at the bottom of the graph.

2. Move your finger up until you touch the top of the bar.

3. Move your finger to the right until you touch the column of inches of rainfall. The number nearest your finger is close to the average rainfall in Phoenix in January. That amount is almost 1 inch.

C. Answer the following questions using the climograph.

1. What is the average temperature in Phoenix in July? _____

2. What is the average rainfall in Phoenix in July? _____

D. Compare Phoenix's average temperature and rainfall in January and July. Would you say that Phoenix has a hot and dry climate, a hot and wet climate, a cool and wet climate, or a cool and dry climate?

January _____

July _____

E. Examine the temperatures and inches of rainfall for Phoenix for all twelve months. Write a brief statement explaining what you see.

_____

_____

Lesson 13

ACTIVITY
Find out the positive and negative effects of building dams in the Southwest.

Damming Wild Rivers

The **BIG** Geographic Question

What are the positive and negative effects of building dams?

In the article you read about the Grand Canyon in the Southwest. In the map skills lesson you discovered how warm and dry states in the Southwest can be. Now study the efforts people have made to bring water to this area through the building of dams.

A. Dams are an important land feature found in many places. Put an **X** beside each statement below that describes how a dam might be used.

_____ To control the water flow of a river so that areas along the river get about the same amount of water

_____ To conserve water for dry periods that may occur throughout the year

_____ As a source of electrical power

B. Look at the map on page 125 of the Almanac and complete the chart below.

Dam	Location	River

C. Find out some reasons that these dams were built. List them on the left side of the chart below. Then find out some problems that have resulted from building these dams in a dry, semi-desert region. List them on the right side of the chart.

Building Dams

PROS (Good Effects)	CONS (Bad Effects)

D. Make a time line that shows the building of major dams in the Southwest. For each dam, mark the year it was completed and the river on which it was built.

1905	1915	1925	1935	1945	1955	1965	1975

E. Think about what you have discovered about dams. Write about the environmental effects—both good and bad—of building dams in the Southwest. Do you think dam building does more good than harm, or more harm than good? Tell what you think and why.

_____

_____

_____

_____

Lesson 14

High and Dry

As you read about the Mountain and Intermontane West region, think about the difficulty of crossing this rugged landscape.

The Mountain West region is a land of extremes. The region covers a huge area, but it has a small population. The region, which includes the states of Idaho, Montana, Wyoming, Nevada, Utah, and Colorado makes up almost one fourth of the land area of the United States. However, fewer than four of every 100 Americans live there.

One reason for the region's sparse population is the ruggedness of the land. Each state in the region has mountain ranges with peaks over two miles high. Many of these are in the Rocky Mountains. The Rockies are about 70 million years old. They rise as high as 14,433 feet above sea level at Mount Elbert in Colorado.

Some of North America's most important rivers start in the Rocky Mountains. The Colorado River and the Rio Grande begin in Colorado, and the Platte begins in Wyoming. The Missouri River starts in the Rocky Mountains of Montana. The direction in which these rivers flow is determined by the **continental divide**, an imaginary line running along the Rocky Mountains.

Rivers on the east side of the divide flow to the Atlantic Ocean by way of the Gulf of Mexico, while rivers on the west side flow to the Pacific Ocean. This means that raindrops that fall only a few feet apart in the Rockies may end up in different oceans thousands of miles apart.

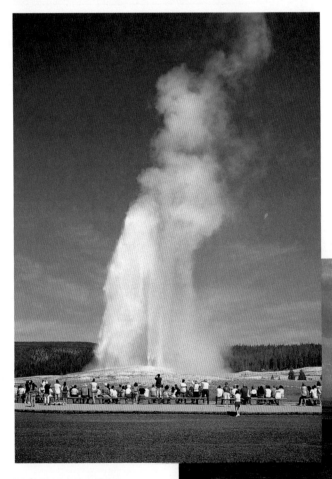

Yellowstone Park in Wyoming has waterfalls, hot springs, and geysers. The most famous is "Old Faithful," which shoots up every 74 minutes.

80

The fact that the Mountain West is an arid, or dry, area despite its many rivers and lakes is another example of the extremes of this region. In fact, Nevada and Utah, part of the Intermontane West, are the two driest states in the United States. The Intermontane West is the area between the Rocky Mountains and the Pacific Coastal Range.

The Great Salt Lake of Utah is one of the natural wonders of the world. Although most lakes contain fresh water, this lake is saltier than ocean water. It is a lake with no outlets, so its water does not drain away. Instead, in the dry climate of the Intermontane West region the water **evaporates,** or changes to a mist, but leaves salt behind. The Bonneville Salt Flats near Salt Lake City, Utah, are an example of what happens when salt builds up and remains in the soil. This flat stretch of salt desert is a favorite spot for land speed trials.

Although the arid, rugged land and salty waters of the Mountain West region seem to have attracted few to live there, more and more people are visiting this land of extremes each year.

The spectacular sandstone pillars of Monument Valley in Utah have been the backdrop for many movies.

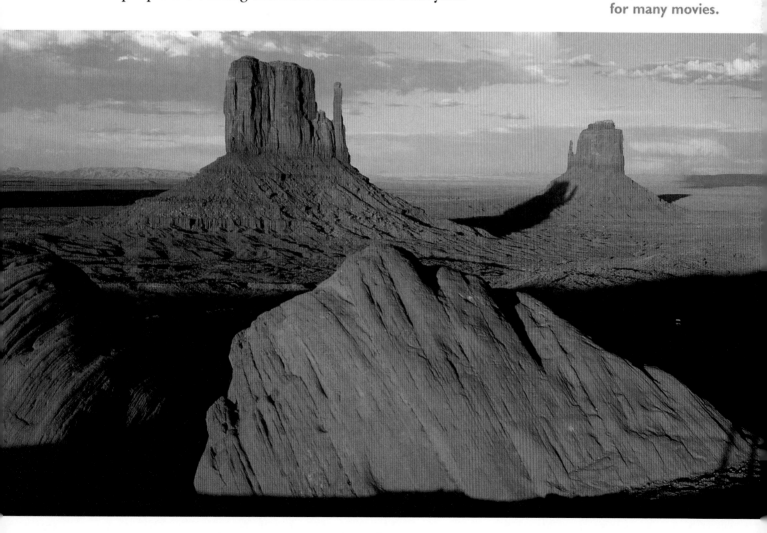

Lesson 14
MAP SKILLS Comparing Maps to Learn About the History of an Area

A historical map shows information about a place's past. A comtemporary map shows information about the present. The maps below show routes used by people traveling west in the past and present.

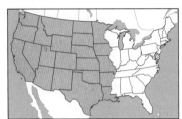

1860s Overland Routes

Map Key

——— Mormon Trail

- - - - Santa Fe Trail

▪▪▪▪ Oregon Trail

——— California Trail

● Cities

1990s Interstate Highway System

Map Key

—(5)— Interstate

● Cities

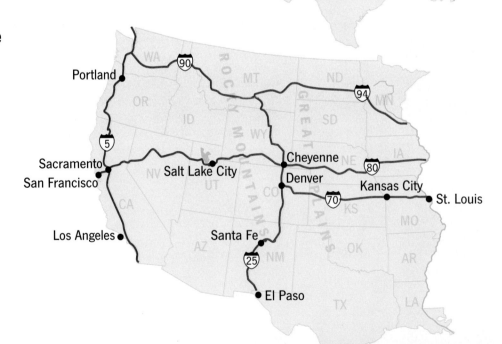

A. Study the 1860 map to find answers to these questions.

1. The routes of the Mormon Trail, the Oregon Trail, and the Sante Fe Trail each followed a river for part of the journey. Why do you think they did this?

_____

2. What major obstacle did each of the trails cross? _____

_____

3. The California Trail split from the Oregon Trail at Fort Hall. Which trail do you think was an easier route to follow?

_____

_____

B. Study the historical 1860s and contemporary 1990s maps to find answers to these questions.

1. People travel across the country a little differently today than they did in 1860. What does the 1990s map tell you about the West today? _____

_____

_____

2. Why would some routes on the contemporary map be the same as

the routes on the historical map? _____

_____

3. Which of the communities on the historical map are also on the

contemporary map? _____

_____

4. Which of the communities on the historical map are not on the

contemporary map? What does this tell you? _____

_____

_____

_____

Lesson 14

ACTIVITY Compare and contrast two urban centers of the West.

Two "Hot" Spots

The **BIG** Geographic Question

What physical and human features have attracted people to two very different desert communities?

In the article you read about the extremes of the Mountain and Intermontane West. The map skills lesson helped you compare past and present travel routes to the West. Now learn what has made two specific communities of the Intermontane West important urban centers.

A. In the Almanac read about the settling of Salt Lake City, Utah, and Las Vegas, Nevada. Use the chart below to help you organize your answers to the following questions.

Question	Salt Lake City, Utah	Las Vegas, Nevada
1. When was it settled?		
2. Who settled it?		
3. Why did they settle there?		

B. Use what you know about the physical features and climate of the region to help you answer these questions.

Question	Salt Lake City, Utah	Las Vegas, Nevada
1. What problems might settlers of this location face?		
2. How did the people of the region overcome the problems?		
3. Were these solutions successful?		

C. Read about the communities today. Think about how they have changed since they were first settled.

Question	Salt Lake City, Utah	Las Vegas, Nevada
1. What things are important to the city today?		
2. What role does tourism play in the community now?		

D. Write a brief article comparing and contrasting the two urban centers of Salt Lake City and Las Vegas. To go with your article, draw a picture to show the differences in the styles of the two communities.

The Diversity of California

As you read about California, notice its many different physical and human features.

California is located in the southwest corner of the United States. It has the most **diverse,** or varied, physical and human features of any state in North America. On its eastern border are the rugged Sierra Nevada mountains. On its western border is the vast Pacific Ocean. In the north stands the active Lassen Peak volcano. The south is dominated by the arid Mojave desert. For many years, the desert and mountains almost cut California off from the rest of the country.

The people of California are as diverse as its land. Over time, the people living in the state have included Native Americans, Spanish explorers, missionaries, Chinese immigrants, and African Americans. Large numbers of Asians and Hispanics are more recent arrivals.

California's mild climate and varied natural scenery have long attracted people from all over the world. However, its Pacific coast location and vast population growth have not come without problems. Two major problems that California faces concern its natural resources and its natural landscape.

The Mojave Desert covers much of southern California.

Earthquakes, which are fairly common in California, can be devastating.

Los Angeles, a city with little water of its own, has a population of over three million. By building a system of aqueducts, or water channels, the city has been able to bring in enough water to keep growing. Water projects have also been important in California's agricultural industry. Much of California's farmland is too dry for growing crops. Irrigation brought water to these areas and made it possible for the state's farmers to lead the country in growing fruits and vegetables.

California has more than a dozen major **faults,** which are fractures or breaks in Earth's crust. The San Andreas Fault, which stretches nearly the length of California's Pacific coast, has been the site of several severe **earthquakes.** An earthquake is a sudden shaking or shock inside Earth that causes movement on its surface. San Francisco, located toward northern California, was hit hard by one in 1906, and by another in 1989. Los Angeles, located toward southern California, had severe earthquakes in 1971 and 1994. These cities were badly damaged but quickly rebuilt.

Nonetheless, the attractions of California are many and just as diverse as its land, people, and problems. For example, Central Valley, located between the Coast Ranges and the Sierra Nevada mountains, is a major agricultural region. Imperial Valley is another important agricultural area located at the southern tip of California, between San Diego and the Colorado River. In contrast, Silicon Valley, which stretches from south of San Francisco through Palo Alto, is where much of today's computer technology is produced. Also, the many movie studios in Hollywood have made Los Angeles the entertainment capital of the world.

California is a state of great wealth and diversity, in terms of land, products, people, and perils. People come from all over the world to California's exciting cities, further adding to the diversity of this region.

Lesson 15
MAP SKILLS Using Physical and Thematic Maps

One of California's biggest problems has been earthquakes that occur along the San Andreas Fault. A fault is a fracture or break in Earth's crust. The San Andreas Fault is one of the most active in the world and is very dangerous. While most faults lie deep beneath Earth's surface, some, like the San Andreas Fault, are visible. It looks like a gash in the land.

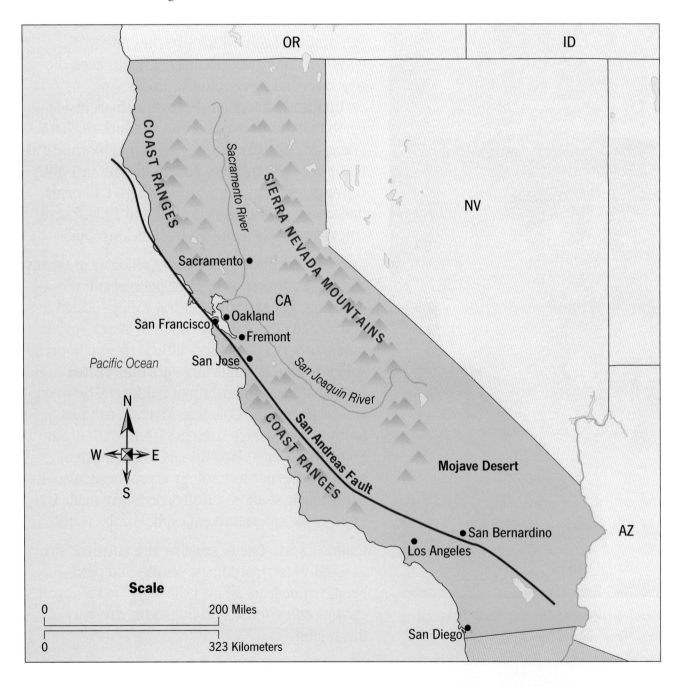

A. Study the physical map of California. Use the information on the map to complete the following.

  1. Trace the line of the San Andreas Fault on the map.

  2. How long is the San Andreas Fault? _____

  3. What major cities are located on or near the fault? _____

  _____

  4. Write a brief desciption of where the fault is located, including where

  it begins and ends. _____

  _____

B. Continue to study the map, particularly the San Andreas Fault. Complete the following.

  1. Which California city has been hit by two severe earthquakes, one

  in 1906 and another in 1989? _____

  _____

  2. Use the chart below to describe the city, including where in California
  it is located and its land and water features.

City Name	
Where It Is Located	
Land and Water Features	

  3. Do you think the city's location makes it more vulnerable to the activity
  of the San Andreas Fault than other cities located along the Fault? Why?

  _____

  4. How does the San Andreas Fault affect life in California? _____

  _____

Lesson 15

ACTIVITY Illustrate the history of water management in California.

Where's the Water?

The BIG Geographic Question — **What are some effects of water management on communities?**

In the article you read about the diversity of California's human and physical features. The map skills lesson focused on the fragile San Andreas Fault in California. Now consider one of the state's other main concerns, the strained water supply. Create a model of California's physical relief to illustrate the location of the state's major efforts to reduce this strain.

A. California has four geographic regions. Find out about the regions. What are their water needs? Copy the following chart onto a sheet of paper. Complete the chart using the Almanac.

Region	Cities	Natural Features	Economic Activities	Source of Water
The Coast				
The Central Valley				
The Mountains				
The Deserts				

B. Use the Almanac to find out about these projects and complete the chart.

Project	Starting Point	Ending Point
Los Angeles Aqueduct		
Colorado River Aqueduct		
Hetch Hetchy Aqueduct		

C. Make your own relief model of California. Mix two parts salt (2 cups) to one part flour (1 cup), and some tap water (3/4 cup) to produce a moldable clay. Mix in a bowl and add 2–3 drops of cooking oil.

1. Plan your map on paper, marking the locations of California's four geographic regions.

2. Transfer the clay mixture to the map. Mold the mountains and other geographic features in relief and allow your model to dry.

3. When the model is completely dry, paint the major regions different colors using tempera or poster paints.

4. Use the information you have gathered from the charts to locate and illustrate the following features on your model:

   • Major urban areas

   • Major agricultural regions

   • Major water projects (dams, aqueducts, and reservoirs)

D. Think about the role water has played in the growth of California's population and industries. What problems do you think California might have with water in the future? What solutions would you recommend?

_____

_____

_____

_____

_____

Lesson 16

As you read about the Pacific Northwest, consider what conditions promote the growth of the lush forests and what happens to them.

For hundreds of years, timber has been an important resource to people who live in the Pacific Northwest. Since the 1500s the people living there have depended on the wood from the forest to build and fuel their homes and to build canoes for traveling.

As the United States grew in the 1800s, it needed more lumber. Loggers went into the woods and chopped down trees. Sawmills cut the logs into boards, which were then shipped all over the country by railroad. By the early 1900s Washington and Oregon were producing huge amounts of lumber for the rest of the country.

Lush forests thrive in the Pacific Northwest states due to the large amount of rainfall they receive. The western side of Washington and Oregon receives up to 130 inches of rain per year in some places. The eastern side, however, is very dry. This difference is due to **orographic precipitation,** which occurs when a flow of warm air is forced upward by a rise in land, such as a hill or mountain.

Cold

Cool

Warm

Rain

Warm

Hot

Dry Lands

Ocean

Moist air moves in from the ocean and flows over the mountain.

Four different systems for cutting timber

Clear-cut

Removes all trees in a large area

Seedcut

Leaves a few trees in an area to provide seeds for a new crop

Shelterwood cut

Leaves a few trees in an area for other trees that need shade to grow

Selective cut

Harvests mature trees to make room for new trees to grow

The lumber industry began to decline in the 1980s when fewer people in the United States built new homes. As a result, there was less demand for lumber. This problem became bigger in later years when wood was replaced by artificial products. Thousands of lumber workers lost their jobs. However, there was a need for lumber in Japan, a country with few timber resources of its own. Ships carried lumber across the Pacific Ocean to Japan, and many jobs were saved.

Another problem for the lumber industry centered around an argument over how to harvest the trees. This debate continues today. For many years, the most widespread method of logging has been **clear-cutting,** using giant sawing machines to strip entire hillsides of trees. The area is then reseeded with a single type of tree. The trees grow and are ready to harvest again in about 70 years.

Although it is efficient, clear-cutting causes **erosion,** the gradual wearing away of the earth. It leaves behind patches that are unsightly. Clear-cutting is also harmful to species of wildlife that inhabit the **old-growth forest,** or forest that has existed for a long time. Some of these animals, including the northern spotted owl, have almost become extinct as their habitat has been destroyed.

Timber in the Pacific Northwest continues to be an important resource. Unfortunately, the use of this resource has become an issue that requires people to weigh heavy consequences and make tough choices.

Lesson 16
MAP SKILLS Using Thematic Maps

In the Pacific Northwest warm, moist air moves in from the Pacific Ocean. As the air reaches the land, it flows up over the Coastal Range of mountains. It then flows down and across the Willamette Valley until it reaches a second, higher range of mountains, the Cascades. Look at the map below.

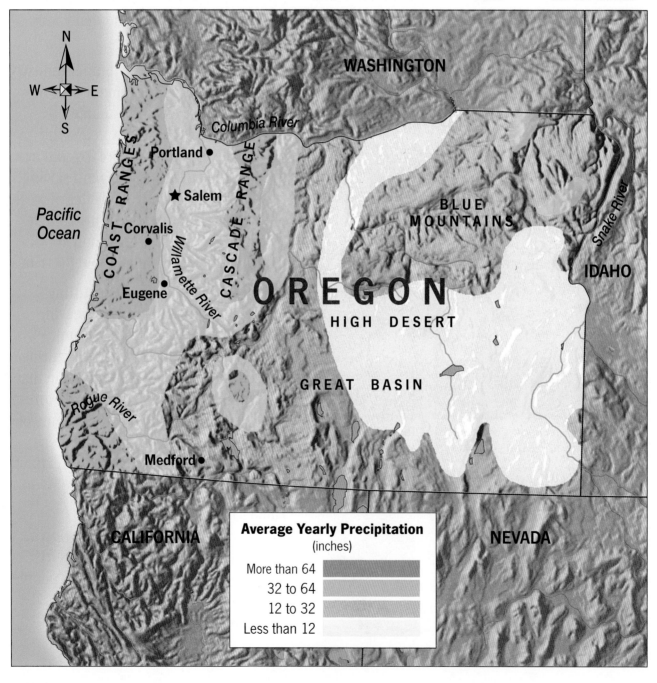

Average Yearly Precipitation (inches)

More than 64
32 to 64
12 to 32
Less than 12

A. Study the map and the precipitation key.

    1. What areas have the highest average precipitation? _____

    2. What physical features are found in or near the areas that have the highest

    precipitation? _____

    3. What areas show the lowest average precipitation? _____

    _____

    4. What physical features are found in the areas that have the lowest

    precipitation? _____

    5. Look back at the diagram of orographic precipitation in the article on
    page 92. Now look at the map of Oregon and the precipitation key.
    Draw the diagram onto the map in the appropriate place.

**B. Look at the map diagram you have created and answer the
following questions.**

    1. What happens to the air as it moves up the ocean side of the mountain?

    _____

    _____

    2. Where does it rain? _____

    _____

    3. What is the air like as it moves down the far side of the mountain?

    _____

    _____

    4. How does this precipitation affect the timber industry in the area?

    _____

    _____

Lesson 16

ACTIVITY Learn to see different sides of an environmental debate.

Depending on Forests

The **BIG**
Geographic Question

How can forest management issues be resolved?

From the article you learned about the vast amounts of timber in the Pacific Northwest and the benefits and problems connected with it. The map skills lesson showed you how the west side of Oregon gets more rain, creating forests on the western side of the state. Now investigate the debate over logging practices in the Pacific Northwest.

A. Answer the following questions about timber.

1. What are some items in your home or school that are made from timber?

_____

_____

2. Where do you think the timber to make these items comes from?

_____

B. Imagine that the items you listed above depended on timber from the Pacific Northwest.

1. How does rainfall affect the growth of trees in this region?

_____

_____

2. What is the most common method of harvesting the trees in the

Pacific Northwest? _____

96

C. Many people disagree over whether or not to harvest trees in the Pacific Northwest. What are some of the advantages of cutting down trees there? What are some of the disadvantages? Put your answers on the chart below.

Advantages	Disadvantages

D. Different groups of people feel strongly about the issue of cutting or not cutting down timber in the Pacific Northwest. Choose one of the following groups of people and think about how they would answer the questions below.

furniture makers

loggers

wildlife scientists

1. How does cutting down timber in the Pacific Northwest affect you?

_____

_____

2. What solutions would you suggest for the issue of cutting or not cutting down the timber?

_____

_____

E. Write a proposal to the United States Secretary of the Interior about this issue. State your view based upon the group that you chose. Take into account how others feel on the issue. What kinds of solutions are there that everyone could agree to?

Lesson 17

Island Treasures

As you read about the Hawaiian Islands, think about how its geography affects the lives of the people who live there.

Hawaii is the only state of our nation that is not located on the North American continent. It is a chain of volcanic islands miles away in the Pacific Ocean. The islands were created by volcanoes that have emerged from the ocean to form Hawaii's mountains.

The first people to live on Hawaii are thought to have traveled 2,500 miles in canoes from the Marquesas Islands, which are located southeast of Hawaii in the Pacific Ocean. About 800 years later more people came from Tahiti. These two Polynesian groups were the islands' native Hawaiians. They lived on the islands for several hundred years.

European explorers and foreigners from many lands began to stop at the Hawaiian Islands as a resting place on their journeys. The islands were seen as a crossroads between the eastern and western hemispheres. Foreigners saw Hawaii's lush vegetation, moderate climate, and ample rainfall as a good place for sugar plantations. When these plantations needed workers, Chinese people looking for jobs immigrated to Hawaii. Japanese and Filipino workers soon followed. Hawaii became a mixture of people from Asia, Europe, North America, and Africa.

The Hawaiian Islands have many active volcanoes.

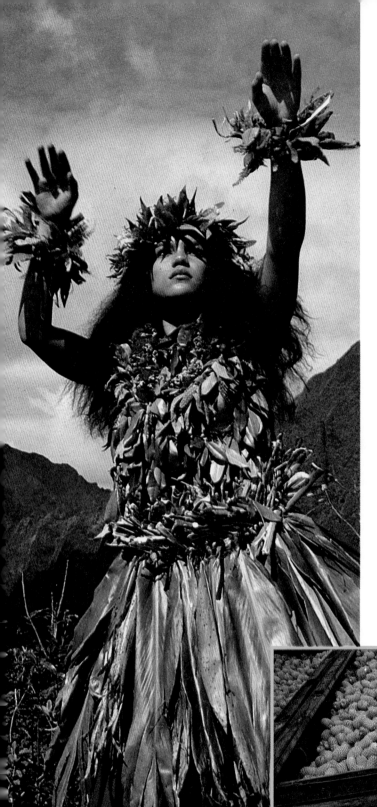

The island of Oahu has nine of the state's ten largest cities and the highest population of any of the Hawaiian Islands. It was named Oahu, which means "gathering place," because in early times the chiefs from the different islands gathered there to meet. Today Hawaii's government meets in the capital city of Honolulu on Oahu. The gathering of the many cultures from East and West can still be seen in Oahu's population today.

Native foods such as *poi,* a starchy food from the stem of the taro plant, and *laulau,* spinach-like chopped taro leaves with fish and pork wrapped in plant leaves, are still very popular. Rice and fruits and vegetables grown on the islands are a major part of the Hawaiian diet. Foods introduced by immigrants reflect the cultural backgrounds of the varied population. Asian, European, and mainland American foods are featured in local Hawaiian supermarkets and restaurants today.

The Hawaiian Islands are best known for their location and climate. But the many different people who have inhabited its lands have influenced these treasured islands.

Pineapples are one of the main crops grown in Hawaii.

Lesson 17
MAP SKILLS Using Maps to Learn About Population

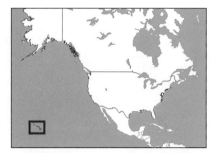

A **census** is a count of the people living in the United States. It is done every ten years. **Population density** means the concentration of people living in a particular area. The map below uses colors to show the population density of Hawaii according to the 1990 census.

Population Density of the Hawaiian Islands

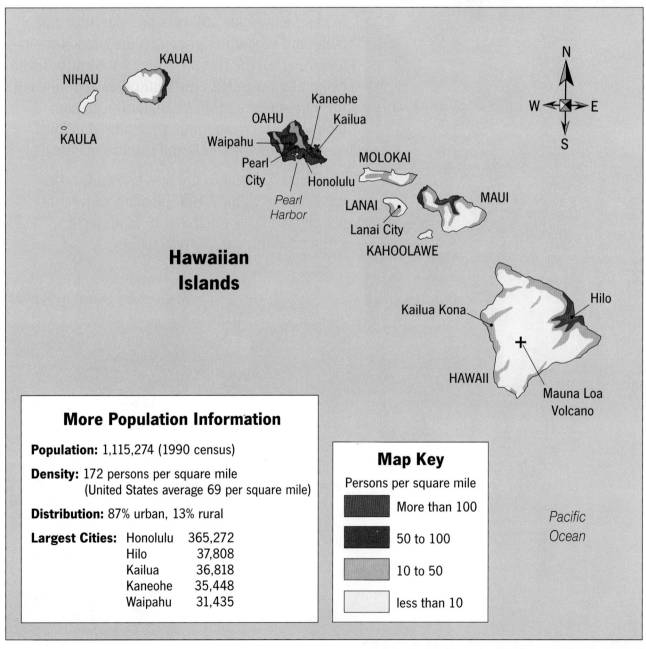

NIHAU

KAUAI

KAULA

OAHU
Waipahu
Pearl
City

Kaneohe
Kailua

Honolulu

Pearl
Harbor

MOLOKAI

LANAI

Lanai City

MAUI

KAHOOLAWE

N
W   E
S

Hawaiian
Islands

Kailua Kona

Hilo

HAWAII

Mauna Loa
Volcano

More Population Information

Population: 1,115,274 (1990 census)

Density: 172 persons per square mile
(United States average 69 per square mile)

Distribution: 87% urban, 13% rural

Largest Cities:

Honolulu	365,272
Hilo	37,808
Kailua	36,818
Kaneohe	35,448
Waipahu	31,435

Map Key
Persons per square mile

More than 100

50 to 100

10 to 50

less than 10

Pacific
Ocean

100

A. Look at the map and answer the questions below.

1. List the nine islands that make up the state of Hawaii.

a. _____   f. _____

b. _____   g. _____

c. _____   h. _____

d. _____   i. _____

e. _____

2. Which color on the map represents the highest density, or concentration of people?

_____

3. Which color represents the sparsely populated areas—areas with the fewest people?

_____

B. *Urban* means "in, of, or like a city." *Rural* means "in, of, or like the country." Use the map to answer the following questions.

1. Which map color would you say best represents urban areas? _____

2. Which color would you say best represents rural areas? _____

3. How many people per square mile live on the northern tip of the

island of Hawaii? _____

4. How do the coasts of the islands compare to the inland areas in population?

_____

5. Which Hawaiian island has the highest population? _____

6. On which island are most of the cities located? _____

7. Compare the city locations with the population density and note your

observations. _____

_____

Lesson 17

ACTIVITY Discover how people have changed Hawaii's ecosystem.

People Causing Change

The **BIG** Geographic Question

How did people change the plant and animal life on Hawaii?

From the article you learned that people from many cultures settled on the Hawaiian Islands. The map skills lesson showed the population densities of the islands. Now find out how people have affected the landscape of Hawaii.

A. The ecosystem of Hawaii includes many living things that are not found anywhere else on Earth. Use the Almanac to find information about the unique life-forms of Hawaii, past and present, and about the effects people have had on the ecosystem.

1. List some of Hawaii's unique plants and animals below. Circle any that

   are endangered. _____

   _____

   _____

   _____

2. Why do you think the ecosystem of Hawaii is unique? _____

   _____

   _____

   _____

   _____

B. Use what you have learned to complete the chart below. Tell how the climate affects each feature and how that feature affects the ecosystem. Add other features you have learned about.

Economic Activity	How Affected by Climate	Effect on Hawaii's Ecosystem
sugarcane plantations		
pineapple plantations		

C. Use the Almanac to find out where pineapples and sugarcane are grown in Hawaii. Then trace or draw a map of Hawaii and place symbols on the map to show the locations of the pineapples and sugarcane. Remember to draw a map key for your symbols.

D. Write a few sentences explaining the effects of human actions on Hawaii's ecosystem.

_____

_____

_____

_____

_____

_____

Lesson 18

Journeying to Alaska

As you read about the geography of Alaska, think about how important it was to develop new forms of transportation and communication.

Alaska is so far north that almost one third of the state lies north of the Arctic Circle. Alaska has a very cold climate and two major mountain ranges. These conditions make it difficult to construct roads and highways there.

The Alaska Highway was built by the United States government during World War II to provide a land route for military equipment. The Dalton Highway was built in the early 1980s. It followed the route of the Trans-Alaska Pipeline. The pipeline was built to carry oil from Prudhoe Bay in northern Alaska to the port of Valdez in the south.

Other than on highways, land travel involves using dogsleds and ATVs (all-terrain vehicles). Dogsleds are one of the earliest means of transportation used by the native Alaskans—the Aleut and Inuit peoples. Today ATVs and snowmobiles are becoming more popular.

Highways have made a difference in Alaska, but airplanes have made an even greater impact. The airplane was introduced to Alaska around 1920. Airplanes brought news and supplies to areas that had little or no connection to the rest of the world. Smaller planes that land on water and planes with special protection from the harsh weather can reach isolated areas. Pilots who fly small airplanes to remote areas are known as bush pilots. They fly to every corner of the state.

Bush pilots often have no runways, so they land on glaciers or lakes. The people in these remote areas appreciate the service these pilots provide in transporting mail, people, and supplies.

Trans-Alaska Pipeline

Another means of transportation in Alaska is the state-owned Alaskan Railroad. It is used to transport materials and manufactured goods from the port cities of Seward and Whittier to Fairbanks and Anchorage, two of the state's largest cities. The Alaskan Railroad also operates passenger trains.

The building of highways in Alaska has connected cities and people to each other. The developments in transportation have made travel and communication easier for people in even the most remote of regions.

As transportation and communication were developed, more people came to Alaska. The Aleut and Inuit began to realize that they were losing control of their homeland. In 1966 these groups came together to form the Alaskan Federation of Natives. They tried to reclaim the 280 million acres of land that belonged to their ancestors. The Alaska Native Claims Settlement Act of 1971 gave back to the native people 44 million acres of land and nearly $1 billion.

Some Alaskans still rely on dogsleds as transportation.

Lesson 18
MAP SKILLS Identifying Various Types of Lines on a Map

Maps that show boundary lines are called **political maps.**
Political maps can show cities, towns, highways, and
sometimes other features such as ferry routes, agricultural
areas, and military bases. Political maps can also show
international boundaries between different countries.

Arctic Ocean

RUSSIA

Prudhoe Bay

Bering Strait

Trans-Alaska Pipeline

Dalton Highway

Arctic Circle

Nome

Livengood
College
Fairbanks

CANADA
Dawson
Delta Junction

Bering Sea

Yukon River

Kuskokwim River

Alaskan R.R.

Mount
McKinley
20,320
feet

Tanana River

Alaska Highway

Bethel

Anchorage
Valdez
Whittier

Seward

N
W E
S

Gulf of Alaska

Juneau

ALEUTIAN
ISLANDS

Pacific Ocean

Scale
0   300 Miles

0   300 Kilometers

Legend
—— River   Mountain
········ Railroad   ★ Capital
—— Pipeline   ● City
══ Alaska Highway
– – – Dalton Highway

A. Look at the map and identify the following features.

   1. Find an international boundary line and trace it with a red line.

   2. Find the highway line and trace it with a yellow line.

   3. Find the railroad line and trace it with a blue line.

   4. Find the Trans-Alaska Pipeline and trace it with a green line.

B. Look at the legend on the map. Find these symbols and write what each one stands for.

   1. ''''''' _____

   2. ——— _____

   3. - - - - _____

   4. ‿ _____

C. Use the map to answer these questions about international boundaries.

   1. What country borders the east side of Alaska? _____

   2. How can you tell the boundary line between Alaska and that country? _____

   _____

   3. What country borders the west side of Alaska?_____

   4. What body of water forms a boundary between Alaska and that country? _____

   _____

D. Think about the boundaries between Alaska and Canada and Alaska and Russia. Write a few sentences explaining which is a physical boundary and which is a human boundary. Explain your answer.

   _____

   _____

   _____

Lesson 18

ACTIVITY Find out how communication and transportation can affect people.

Saving the Land

The **BIG** Geographic Question

How have the lives of native Alaskans been affected by transportation and communication developments?

From the article you learned that as more ways of traveling to and in Alaska came about, more people went there. The map skills lesson showed how different lines on a map represent features of Alaska. Now find out what happened with the land in Alaska.

A. Use the information in the article, map skills lesson, and Almanac to complete the following about Alaska.

1. Describe the land of Alaska?

   _____

   _____

2. Who are the native people of Alaska?

   _____

   _____

3. How do the native people usually travel in Alaska?

   _____

   _____

4. How has the land of Alaska been used to connect it to other places?

   _____

   _____

   _____

B. Review the information you learned about why the native Alaskans wanted to reclaim land and how the United States government responded to their claims. Organize the information you find on the chart below.

People	Actions Regarding Land in Alaska
Native Alaskans' claims	
United States government's response	

C. Use what you have learned from the activity and the Almanac to role-play with a partner how you might have decided to divide the land and cash. Then write a short paragraph below describing your decision. Include a description of how your decision compares to what the Native Alaskans decided to do.

_____

_____

_____

_____

_____

_____

_____

_____

_____

_____

ALMANAC

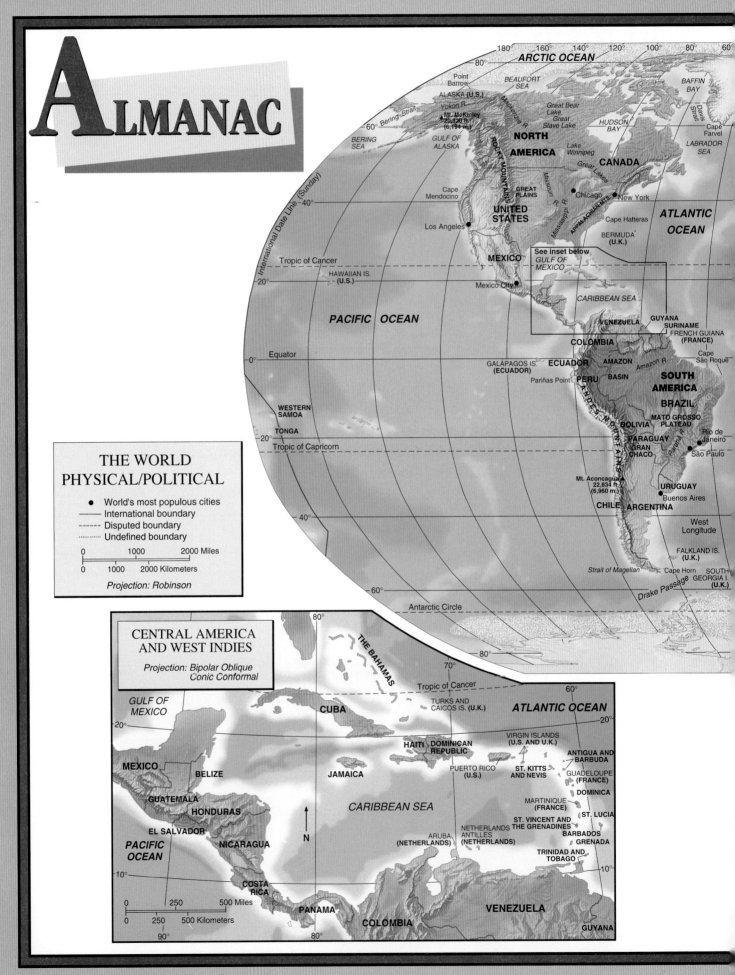

THE WORLD
PHYSICAL/POLITICAL

- ● World's most populous cities
- —— International boundary
- ----- Disputed boundary
- ········· Undefined boundary

| 0 | 1000 | 2000 Miles |
| 0 | 1000 | 2000 Kilometers |

Projection: Robinson

CENTRAL AMERICA AND WEST INDIES

Projection: Bipolar Oblique Conic Conformal

| 0 | 250 | 500 Miles |
| 0 | 250 | 500 Kilometers |

ARCTIC OCEAN

20° 0° 20° 40° 60° 80° 100° 120° 140° 160° 180°

NAAT
GREENLAND
SEA
JAN MAYEN
(NORWAY)
SVALBARD IS.
(NORWAY)
NORWEGIAN
SEA
North Cape
Cape
Zelaniya
KARA SEA
LAPTEV SEA
EAST
SIBERIAN SEA
FRANZ JOSEF IS.
(RUSSIA)
BARENTS
SEA
VERKHOYANSK
RANGE
80°
OE IS.
MARK)
Arctic Circle
NORTH
SEA
See Inset below
Lake Ladoga
SIBERIA
WEST
SIBERIAN
PLAIN
Ob R.
Yenisey R.
CENTRAL
SIBERIAN
PLATEAU
Lena R.
ASIA
SEA OF
OKHOTSK
Cape
Lopatka
60°
esterre
EUROPE
ALPS
NORTH
EUROPEAN PLAIN
RUSSIA
Lake
Baikal
YABLONOV
RANGE
KURIL IS.
(RUSSIA)
S.
AL)
Danube R.
Volga R.
URAL MOUNTAINS
Mt. Elbrus
18,510 ft.
(5,642 m.)
CASPIAN
DEPRESSION
KAZAKSTAN
ALTAI MTNS.
MONGOLIA
Changchun
Shenyang
SEA
OF
JAPAN
JAPAN
40°
BLACK SEA
GEORGIA
ARMENIA
CASPIAN SEA
ARAL
SEA
UZBEKISTAN
KYRGYZSTAN
TIANSHAN
GOBI
Beijing
Tianjin
NORTH
KOREA
Seoul
SOUTH
KOREA
Tokyo
ROCCO
TURKEY
LEBANON
SYRIA
IRAQ
AZERBAIJAN
TURKMENISTAN
TAJIKISTAN
TAKLIMAKAN
CHINA
Mt. Everest
29,028 ft.
(8,848 m.)
Chongqing
Wuhan
EAST
CHINA
SEA
Shanghai
ATLAS MOUNTAINS
MEDITERRANEAN SEA
ISRAEL
JORDAN
IRAN
PLATEAU
OF IRAN
AFGHANISTAN
HIMALAYAS
NEPAL
BHUTAN
Chang Jiang
Yangtze R.
TAIWAN
Tropic of Cancer
20°
TUNISIA
ALGERIA
LIBYA
EGYPT
QATTARA
DEPRESSION
Cairo
Nile R.
KUWAIT
BAHRAIN
QATAR
UNITED
ARAB
EMIRATES
PAKISTAN
Delhi
Ganges R.
INDIA
BANGLADESH
Calcutta
MYANMAR
LAOS
HONG KONG
MACAO (PORTUGAL)
MARSHALL ISLANDS
SAHARA
SAUDI
ARABIA
OMAN
Mumbai
(Bombay)
BAY OF
BENGAL
THAILAND
SOUTH
CHINA
SEA
Manila
GUAM (U.S.)
TANIA
MALI
NIGER
CHAD
SUDAN
ERITREA
YEMEN
DJIBOUTI
ARABIAN
SEA
Cape Asir
Cape Comorin
SRI
LANKA
VIETNAM
CAMBODIA
BRUNEI
PHILIPPINES
FEDERATED STATES
OF MICRONESIA
NEA
GHANA
NIGERIA
BENIN
AFRICA
CENTRAL
AFRICAN REP.
ETHIOPIA
ETHIOPIAN
HIGHLANDS
SOMALIA
MALDIVES
SINGAPORE
MALAYSIA
PALAU
KIRIBATI
I'VOIRE
OME AND PRÍNCIPE
EQUATORIAL GUINEA
TOGO CAMEROON
GABON
CONGO
Zaire R.
CONGO
(ZAIRE)
BASIN
RWANDA
UGANDA
KENYA
Lake
Victoria
BURUNDI
Kilimanjaro
19,340 ft.
(5,895 m.)
SEYCHELLES
Jakarta
INDONESIA
PAPUA
NEW
GUINEA
SOLOMON
ISLANDS
NAURU
Equator
0°
MA
ANGOLA
ZAMBIA
MALAWI
TANZANIA
COMOROS
MADAGASCAR
MAURITIUS
INDIAN
OCEAN
COCOS IS.
(AUSTRALIA)
Cape
York
CORAL
SEA
TUVALU
VANUATU
FIJI
NAMIBIA
BOTSWANA
ZIMBABWE
MOZAMBIQUE
Mozambique Channel
RÉUNION
(FRANCE)
Tropic of Capricorn
WESTERN
PLATEAU
AUSTRALIA
GREAT DIVIDING RANGE
NEW
CALEDONIA
(FRANCE)
20°
TLANTIC
OCEAN
SOUTH
AFRICA
SWAZILAND
LESOTHO
Cape of
Good Hope
East
Longitude
Prime Meridian
N
KERGUELEN IS.
(FRANCE)
Mt. Kosciusko
7,310 ft.
(2,228 m.)
TASMAN
SEA
NEW
ZEALAND
40°
Antarctic Circle
60°
80°
ANTARCTICA

EUROPE
Projection: Azimuthal
Equal Area

FINLAND
NORWAY
SWEDEN
St. Petersburg
10°
0°
IRELAND
UNITED
KINGDOM
DENMARK
ESTONIA
Moscow
50°
N
ATLANTIC
OCEAN
London
NETHERLANDS
BELGIUM
LUXEMBOURG
GERMANY
POLAND
LATVIA
LITHUANIA
RUSSIA
BELARUS
RUSSIA
Paris
FRANCE
CZECH
REPUBLIC
SLOVAKIA
UKRAINE
10°
40°
SWITZERLAND
AUSTRIA
HUNGARY
SLOVENIA
CROATIA
MOLDOVA
PORTUGAL
SPAIN
ITALY
BOSNIA
HERZEGOVINA
SERBIA
YUGOSLAVIA
MONTENEGRO
ROMANIA
BULGARIA
BLACK SEA
GEORGIA
GIBRALTAR
(U.K.)
MEDITERRANEAN
ALBANIA
MACEDONIA
GREECE
TURKEY
0 250 500 Miles
0 250 500 Kilometers
TUNISIA
MALTA
SEA
20°
CYPRUS
SYRIA
30°
LEBANON

111

ATLANTIC OCEAN

BE
(U.

Tropic

Philadelphia
Baltimore
⊛ Washington
Norfolk
Cape Hatteras

APPALACHIAN

COASTAL PLAIN

THE BAHAMAS

Nassau ⊛

TURKS AND
CAICOS IS.
(U.K.)

DOMINICAN
REPUBLIC

⊛ Santo
Domingo

PU
RI

GUA

HAITI

Port-au-
Prince

ST. VINCENT AND

TRI

NETH

S
AM

Cleveland
Columbus
Pittsburgh
Cincinnati
Indianapolis

Tennessee R.

Miami

Jacksonville

Atlanta

Tampa

Straits of Florida

CUBA

Camagüey

Havana

Santiago de Cuba

JAMAICA

Kingston

CAYMAN IS.
(U.K.)

CARIBBEAN SEA

ARUBA (NETH.)

Cape Gracias
a Dios

GULF
OF
PANAMA

PANAMÁ

80°

Chicago
Des Moines

Ohio R.

St. Louis

Memphis

OZARK
PLATEAU

Mississippi River

New Orleans

GULF OF MEXICO

Yucatán
Channel

Cape
Catoche

Mérida

YUCATÁN PEN.

BELIZE

GULF OF
HONDURAS

San Pedro Sula

HONDURAS

NICARAGUA

Lake
Nicaragua

COSTA RICA

PANAMA

CENTRAL AMERICA

Equator

90°

uri

River

Kansas City

Houston

Tampico

CAMPECHE BAY

Veracruz

Citlaltépetl
18,700 ft.
(5,700 m.)

EL SALVADOR

GUATEMALA

⊛ GUATEMALA

Omaha
Denver
Platte R.
Arkansas

Red
R.

Dallas

Fort Worth

Santa Fe

San
Antonio

Rio
Grande

Puebla
Mexico City ⊛

León

MEXICO

SIERRA MADRE
ORIENTAL

Monterrey

MEXICAN
PLATEAU

Balsas R.

Acapulco

100°

COLORADO
PLATEAU

Phoenix

El Paso

Ciudad Juárez

Chihuahua

Rio

SIERRA MADRE OCCIDENTAL

Guadalajara

N

⟵

BASIN

Death Valley
-282 ft.
(-89 m.)

Grand
Canyon

Colorado

GULF OF CALIFORNIA

BAJA CALIFORNIA PEN.

Cape San Lucas

REVILLAGIGEDO IS.
(MEX.)

110°

NEVADA

Mt. Whitney
14,494 ft.
(4,418 m.)

San
Salt
Lake

San Francisco

San Jose

Los Angeles

San Diego

Tijuana

GUADALUPE I.
(MEX.)

120°

San Juárez

AINS

Salt
Lake
City

Cape Flattery

Juan de Fuca
Strait
Pugot
Sound
Seattle
Tacoma
Olympia

F.D.
Roosevelt
Lake

COLUMBIA

Pend Oreille
Lake

Flathead
Lake

Missouri   River

Fort Peck
Lake

Lake
Sakakawea

MONTANA

NORTH DAKOTA

★Bismarck

Mt. Rainier
14,410 ft.
(4,392 m.)

Portland ●

Columbia   River

PLATEAU

WASHINGTON

Helena
★

Yellowstone   R.

Lake
Oahe

Salem
★

▲ Mt. Hood
11,235 ft.
(3,424 m.)

CASCADE RANGE

BITTERROOT RANGE

ROCKY

BIGHORN
MTS.

SOUTH DAKOT

★ Pierre

OREGON

IDAHO

Borah Peak
12,662 ft.
(3,859 m.) ▲

Grand Teton
Peak
13,770 ft.
(4,197 m.)

WYOMING

Powder   River

BLACK
HILLS

G
R
E
A
T

Mt. Shasta
14,162 ft.
(4,316 m.) ▲

Boise
★

Continental   Divide

North Platte River

Missouri

NEBRASKA

Cape
Mendocino

Goose Lake

River

Snake   River

GREAT

BASIN

Great
Salt
Lake

GREAT
SALT LAKE
DESERT

RANGE

MOUNTAINS

South Platte River

Cheyenne ★

Platte

Republican   River

Platte

Pyramid
Lake

Salt Lake
City ★

Mt. Elbert
14,433 ft.
(4,399 m.) ▲

Denver ●

P
L
A
I
N
S

KANS

Sacramento

Lake
Tahoe

★ Carson City

Utah
Lake

WASATCH

Green River

Pikes Peak ▲
14,110 ft.
(4,301 m.)

Sacramento ★

NEVADA

SIERRA

Mono Lake

San
Francisco
Oakland
San
Jose

Joaquin

● Fresno

NEVADA

CALIFORNIA

Mt. Whitney
14,494 ft.
(4,418 m.) ▲

Death Valley
−282 ft.
(−89 m.)

Las Vegas ●

Lake
Mead

UTAH

PAINTED
DESERT

COLORADO

Arkansas

River

COLORADO
PLATEAU

Lake
Powell

Divide

SANGRE DE CRISTO MTS.

★ Santa Fe

Canadian

River

OKLAHO

Oklahoma C

Point
Conception

MOJAVE DESERT

River

Colorado

Grand
Canyon

Rio   Grande

NEW

San

PACIFIC

Los Angeles
San Bernardino
Riverside

Continental

MEXICO

LLANO

Red

River

OCEAN

Long
Beach

Salton
Sea

● Glendale
Phoenix ●
Mesa ●

ARIZONA

Gila   River

Divide

ESTACADO

Brazos

River

● San Diego

Tucson ●

Rio

TEXAS

Fort W

El Paso ●

Pecos

River

Colorado   River

160°   155°

EDWARDS
PLATEAU

Aus

Kauai
Channel

HAWAII

RUSSIA

180°   170°   70°

Pt.
Barrow

150°

Rio   San Antonio ●

Honolulu ★

PACIFIC OCEAN

Alenuihaha
Channel

Arctic Circle

BROOKS RANGE

ALASKA

Grande

20°   20°

Bering Strait

SEWARD
PEN.

Yukon   River

Tanana

0   100 Miles

Mauna Kea
13,796 ft.
(4,205 m.) ▲

CANADA

MEXICO

0   100 Kilometers

160°   155°

Mt. McKinley
20,320 ft.
(6,194 m.) ▲

River

60°

25°

170°

BERING

0   250   500 Miles

Iliamna
Lake

ALASKA

RANGE

Juneau ★

0   250   500 Kilometers

BRISTOL
BAY

ALASKA PENINSULA

GULF OF
ALASKA

SEA

50°

ALEUTIAN ISLANDS

Shellkof Str.

140°

60°

180°   170°   160°   150°

130°

PACIFIC

OCEAN

GULF
OF
CALIFORNIA

45°

40°

35°

125°

30°

120°   115°   110°   105°   100°

114

CANADA

Lake of the Woods

Red Lake

Lake Superior

St. Lawrence River

MAINE

Moosehead Lake

MICHIGAN

MINNESOTA

WISCONSIN

Minneapolis St. Paul ★

Mississippi River

Lake Huron

Lake Michigan

Grand Rapids

Milwaukee

Madison

Lansing

Detroit

Niagara Falls

Lake Ontario

Rochester

Buffalo

Lake Erie

Cleveland

Toledo

Akron

Canton

Pittsburgh

ADIRONDACK MTNS.

Lake Champlain

Mt. Washington 6,288 ft. (1,905 m.) ★ Augusta

Montpelier

N.H.

VT.

★ Concord

Albany

Hudson R.

Boston ★ MASS.

Cape Cod

Hartford

Providence

New Haven

R.I.

CONN.

Syracuse

NEW YORK

Susquehanna River

Newark

Newark

New York

PENNSYLVANIA

N.J.

Youngstown

Philadelphia

Trenton

Harrisburg

Camden

IOWA

Omaha

Des Moines ★

ILLINOIS

Chicago

Gary

Hammond

OHIO

Columbus

Dayton

Dover

MD.

Baltimore

DELAWARE BAY

DEL.

CENTRAL

LOWLAND

Springfield ★

Indianapolis ★

INDIANA

Cincinnati River

Annapolis

Washington

D.C.

Kansas City

Jefferson City ★

Topeka ★

Kansas City

St. Louis

East St. Louis

Wabash R.

Ohio R.

Frankfort

Louisville

KENTUCKY

WEST VIRGINIA

Charleston

Richmond

Newport News

VIRGINIA

Norfolk

CHESAPEAKE BAY

ATLANTIC

OCEAN

Harry S. Truman Res.

MISSOURI

OZARK PLATEAU

Cumberland River

Raleigh

Roanoke River

APPALACHIAN MOUNTAINS

Tulsa

R.S. Kerr Res.

ARKANSAS

OZARK PLATEAU

Memphis

Mississippi River

Knoxville

★ Nashville

TENNESSEE

PLATEAU

Mt. Mitchell 6,684 ft. (2,037 m.)

Winston-Salem

NORTH CAROLINA

Cape Hatteras

Lake Eufaula

Little Rock ★

Tennessee R.

CUMBERLAND R.

★ Columbia

SOUTH CAROLINA

ke xoma

Dallas

Birmingham

Chattahoochee R.

Atlanta

GEORGIA

COASTAL

PLAIN

UNITED STATES

⊛ National capital

★ State capital

● Major city

━━ International boundary

─── State boundary

0   150   300 Miles

0   150   300 Kilometers

Projection: Albers Equal Area

LOUISIANA

★ Jackson

ALABAMA

Montgomery

Alabama R.

Toledo Bend Res.

Sam Rayburn Reservoir

MISSISSIPPI

Lake Pontchartrain

Baton Rouge ★

★ Tallahassee

Jacksonville

FLORIDA

Houston

New Orleans

Orlando

Cape Canaveral

GULF OF MEXICO

N

Tampa

St. Petersburg

Lake Okeechobee

Miami

Cape Sable

Key West

Straits of Florida

THE BAHAMAS

CUBA

95°   90°   85°   80°   75°

45°

65°

40°

35°

70°

30°

25°

The Northeast Region Today	
Agriculture	supplies local cities with produce such as vegetables, poultry, and dairy products; not a major producer of farm goods for the rest of the United States due to thin soils
Industry	manufactures electronic equipment, electrical machinery, tools, textiles, chemicals, and iron and steel; fishing, printing and publishing, chemical engineering, and medical research are additional industries
Movement	some Asian and Latin American immigrants arriving; people moving to the suburbs instead of living in the city; city governments trying to attract people and businesses back to urban areas by repairing old buildings and building new parks and malls

Source: *Geography and Development: A World Regional Approach,* James Fisher, 1989

Alaska Native Claims Settlement Act, 1971

Native Alaskans (Inuits and Aleuts) lost much of their land as new people settled Alaska. Their ancestors' goals were to reclaim the lost land and govern themselves.

In the late 1960s oil was discovered in northern Alaska. The United States wanted to build a pipeline to carry the oil to the lower forty-eight states. Many native Alaskans had claimed the land on which the pipeline would run. The United States government passed the Alaska Native Claims Settlement Act in 1971. The native Alaskans received 44 million acres of land and $962.5 million. Twelve regions were set up in which the native Alaskans could govern themselves. These regions, or corporations, were organized around similar cultures. Each native was a stockholder of the corporation. In return, the United States government was able to build the oil pipeline.

Source: *Alaska: A to Z,* Angela Herb, 1993

Population Density of the Middle Atlantic States, 1990

Persons per
square mile

More than 250

100 to 250

Less than 100

Adirondack
Mountain
Range

Lake Ontario

Albany ★

Syracuse

Rochester

NY

Catskill
Mountain
Range

Buffalo

Lake
Erie

N

W   E

S

Newark

New York City

PA

APPALACHIAN MOUNTAINS

Susquehanna River

Delaware River

★ Trenton

Harrisburg

Philadelphia

NJ

Pittsburgh

Wilmington

Delaware
Bay

Baltimore

MD

Annapolis

Dover

ATLANTIC OCEAN

DE

Allegheny Mountain Range

Washington, D.C.

Chesapeake
Bay

Source: *World Book Encyclopedia*, 1991

Tourist Attractions of the South

Walt Disney World

People arrive by cars, buses, trains, and planes to visit the many sites at Walt Disney World in Orlando, Florida. Here, people enjoy themselves at places such as the Magic Kingdom, Epcot Center, Adventure Land, and Frontier Land. The hot, humid summers and mild winters make visiting possible year-round. Near Disney World, there are other tourist attractions, such as the Kennedy Space Center, Big Cypress Swamp and the Everglades, and the sandy beaches of Florida.

Civil Rights Monument

The Civil Rights Monument in Montgomery, Alabama, is the home of the Civil Rights Movement of the 1960s, led by Dr. Martin Luther King, Jr. Located at the monument are words from Dr. King's speeches, which are on display. People travel to this historic site using all forms of transportation. The warm summers and mild winters make visiting Montgomery enjoyable, even though the area does receive much rain. People also visit the state capitol building, the Montgomery Zoo, and the Old North Hull Street Historic District, which are near the monument.

Great Smoky Mountains National Park

For nature lovers, the Great Smoky Mountains National Park is the place to visit. Located in Tennessee and North Carolina, one can get to the park by car. Once there, one can hike Rainbow Falls Trail, drive the Blue Ridge Parkway, camp at Cades Cove, or bike along Parson Branch Road. Since humidity is high during the summer, swimming is popular, especially at Sliding Rock. One can also hike the famous Appalachian Trail or visit Chattanooga, to shop or eat at quaint restaurants.

Kennedy Space Center

Kennedy Space Center is located in Cocoa Beach, Florida. It is the home of the rocket complex of the National Aeronautics and Space Administration (NASA). The climate is hot and humid during the summer and the winters are mild, with gentle coastal breezes yearlong. One can visit Spaceport, USA, or take a narrated bus tour. One can also see an IMAX film of space flight or visit the Brevard Museum of History and Natural Science. Cape Canaveral, located along the east-central coast of Florida, includes the Kennedy Space Center and also has tours. People arrive by planes, trains, buses, and cars to see this important center for science and research.

The Everglades National Park and Big Cypress National Preserve

The Everglades National Park and Big Cypress National Preserve are two of Florida's most beautiful physical features. These wetlands, located in southern Florida from Lake Okeechobee to Florida Bay and the Gulf of Mexico, thrive because of the hot summers and mild winters. People arrive by boat, car, and plane to see birds and animals in their natural environment. One can travel the Anhinga Trail, which is a boardwalk that leads into the swamp. It allows visitors to see junglelike plant life, crocodiles, alligators, manatees, huge turtles, and swamp birds. Visitors can also see Fort Jefferson National Monument, Biscayne Bay National Park, and the Florida Keys.

The Appalachian Trail

The Appalachian Trail extends from Mt. Katahdin in Maine to Springer Mountain in Georgia. Because the trail is so long, the climate may be different at each part of the trail that one is visiting. People can travel the trail by car. Along the Appalachian Trail, one can hike or ski. The area is also great for bird-watching.

Historical Peoples of the Southwest

Native American Group	Language and Customs	Food and Agriculture	Shelters and Clothing	Land Area and Climate
Navajo	• similar to the Apache language • sand painting for curing sickness	• hunting and gathering • herding of sheep, cattle, and goats • water source: rivers, lakes or streams	• hogans—houses made of earth and logs • garments made of animal skins	• northwestern New Mexico, Arizona, and southeastern Utah • warm, dry
Hopi	• Hopi language • dances in which snakes were released at the end to ask the Rain God to send rain	• sheepherding • farming: corn, squash, beans • water source: rivers, lakes or streams	• terraced, stone, and adobe apartments • cotton woven into a light-weight cloth	• northeastern Arizona • warm, dry
Pueblo	• Tewa, Zuni, and Keresan languages • dances to ensure good crops	• hunting • farming: corn and cotton • water source: river	• pueblo apartments—mud and stone square structures with many rooms • cotton woven into light-weight cloth	• northern Arizona, western New Mexico, along the Rio Grande • warm, dry

BosWash Megalopolis

Urban Area	Washington, D.C.
State Located	District of Columbia
Population of City	617,000
Major Industries	federal government, tourism, law and accounting, printing and publishing
Physical Features	located where the Chesapeake and Ohio Canal meet the Potomac River
Transportation Links to Other Cities	Dulles International Airport, National Airport, subways, superhighways

Urban Area	New York City
State Located	New York
Population of City	7,352,700
Major Industries	tourism, finance, apparel industry, printing and publishing
Physical Features	located on two islands and at the mouth of the Hudson River
Transportation Links to Other Cities	John F. Kennedy International Airport, Laguardia Airport, Penn Station, Grand Central Station

BosWash Megalopolis

Urban Area	Philadelphia
State Located	Pennsylvania
Population of City	1,647,000
Major Industries	finance, medicine, chemicals, clothing manufacturing
Physical Features	located along the Delaware River which flows into the Atlantic Ocean
Transportation Links to Other Cities	Philadelphia International Airport, Conrail trains, subways

Urban Area	Boston
State Located	Massachusetts
Population of City	577,830
Major Industries	tourism, clothing manufacturing, printing, defense, finance
Physical Features	located along the Charles River, Boston Harbor, and part of the Atlantic Ocean; the Blue Hills to the south and the Middlesex Falls to the north
Transportation Links to Other Cities	Logan International Airport in East Boston, subway system

BosWash Megalopolis

Urban Area	Baltimore
State Located	Maryland
Population of City	736,014
Major Industries	shipbuilding and ship repair, steel manufacturing, scientific research
Physical Features	located at the head of the Patapsco River near Chesapeake Bay
Transportation Links to Other Cities	Friendship International Airport, Harbor Tunnel Thruway, Francis Scott Key Bridge

California Water Projects

The Colorado River Aqueduct

The Colorado River Aqueduct serves the Los Angeles and San Diego area. Its source is the Colorado River at Hoover Dam.

The Los Angeles Aqueduct

The Los Angeles Aqueduct's source is the Owens River in the Sierra Nevada Range. This aqueduct supplies water to the city of Los Angeles.

The Hetch Hetchy Aqueduct

The Hetch Hetchy Aqueduct supplies water to the San Francisco Bay area. Its source is the Tuolumne River in the Sierra Nevada Range in eastern California.

Sources: *The World Almanac and Book of Facts*, Robert Famighetti, editor, 1995;
1996 Information Please Almanac, Otto Johnson, editor, 1995;
Regional Geography of the United States, Tom McKnight, 1992

Salt Lake City, Utah

History	Fleeing religious persecution in Illinois, the Mormons settled in Salt Lake City in July of 1847. The hot and dry desert climate in Salt Lake City made living there very hard. In the summer of 1848, crickets began eating the Mormons' crops, almost destroying them. The crops were saved by sea gulls from the great Salt Lake that swooped down and ate the crickets. In Salt Lake City, finding fresh water was a problem, also. Water was eventually piped in from other places for the crops and the people.
Today	Today, Salt Lake City is Utah's largest city. Industries such as steel and oil refining are important. Other economic activities that are important to Salt Lake City are copper mining, sugar refining, and high-tech firms, including research for the defense industry. The city is the center of the Mormon Church and serves as the center of government for Utah. It is the planned next site of the Winter Olympics.

Las Vegas, Nevada

History	Las Vegas, founded in 1905, was originally a mining town. It became a thriving city with the help of the Union Pacific Railroad. The hot and dry climate made living in the area hard. Because the water supply in Las Vegas was very low, many dams were built to bring water into the city. This helped the west-central region of the state develop into an important agricultural area. The dams brought many people to the city to work and live. Many hotels were built to house them. In 1931, gambling was legalized, leading to the growth of casinos.
Today	Today, tourism is the major industry in Las Vegas due to the hundreds of casinos, restaurants, and hotels located in the city. This has made Las Vegas Nevada's largest city.

Source: *Cities of the United States, The West*, Gale Research, 1989

Dams of the Southwest

Hoover Dam

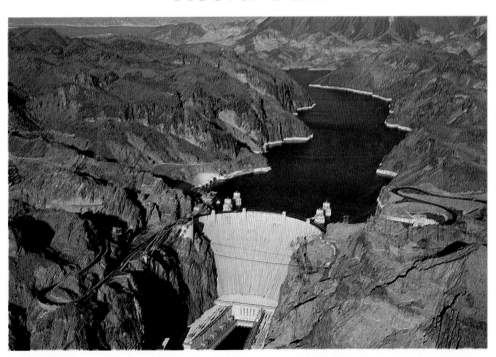

Facts about Dams of the Southwest

	Hoover Dam	Elephant Butte Dam	Glen Canyon Dam
River	Colorado River	Rio Grande	Colorado River
Location	Arizona-Nevada border	New Mexico	Arizona-Utah border
Year	1936	1916	1964
Purpose	• supplies electricity to the Pacific southwest; supplies southern California farms with water	• provides water for irrigation for cotton, grapes, and pecans in the southwest	• supplies water and electricity to Rocky Mountain states; prevents Colorado River from flooding

Environmental Problems

Several environmental problems have occurred since the construction of many dams in the United States. Controlling the flow of water is a problem. When a river's waters do not flow quickly, sand and soil settle to the bottom of the river. Fish that need a clean river bed to lay their eggs have no place to reproduce.

Another problem is the loss of important wildlife habitats. As water flows into the reservoir, the sand, stones, and dirt that it carried settle to the bottom. None of this material is emptied at the river's mouth. Sandbars and islands do not form in the river so many birds and fish have no place to feed or nest.

Finally, changes in plant life have affected the wildlife in the area. The changes in water level have destroyed natural growth patterns and types of plants. Many animals and fish that have depended on these plants as food are dying because their food sources are gone.

Sources: "The Trouble with Dams," Robert Devine, *Atlantic Monthly,* August, 1995
World Book Encyclopedia, 1991

Hawaii's Ecosystem

	Native to Hawaii	From Other Regions
Birds	• nene, or Hawaiian Goose (was near extinction but has been preserved) • Hawaiian stilt (endangered)	• crested honeycreeper (endangered) • Hawaiian coot (endangered) • myna, sparrow, cardinal
Animals	• hoary bat • Hawaiian monk seal	• dog, cow, goat, sheep, deer, horse, mongoose
Plants/Flowers	• coconut, breadfruit tree, bamboo, banana, sugarcane, sandalwood	• mango, papaya, avocado, pineapple, evergreen tree, eucalyptus

Hawaii's Main Products

Product	Location	Climate	Effect on the Land
Pineapples	• central Molokai • Lanai • Oahu (central valley)	• warm, moist climate and well-drained soil needed	• Streams that were shifted to support crops have prevented fish such as gobies from swimming to the ocean to reproduce.
Sugarcane	• Hawaii (northeast/southeast) • Maui (central/northwest) • Oahu (central valley)	• much rainfall needed (80–120") • temperature range between 75° and 86°	• Wildlife habitat was destroyed in order to build large plantations.

Sources: *World Book Encyclopedia,* 1991
Nature in Danger: Threatened Habitats and Species, Noel Simon, 1995
Hawaii Handbook, J.D. Bisignani, 1990

States of the New England Region

Maine

Vegetation	• pine, spruce, fir, sugar maple
Wildlife	• moose, whales, lobsters, black bears
Natural Resources	• soil: sand in coastal areas, clay in lowlands, and gravel-like soils in higher elevations; products include apples, potatoes, blueberries, and livestock • minerals: granite and limestone in southern Maine; slate in central Maine; other minerals such as copper, zinc, and silver • 90% of state is forested

New Hampshire

Vegetation	• ash, birch, cedar
Wildlife	• deer, black bears, ruffed grouse, beavers
Natural Resources	• soil: richest in valleys; products include dairy products, hay, apples, berries, maple syrup • minerals: gravel and sand used for roadbuilding materials • 80% of state is forested

Massachusetts

Vegetation	• eastern white and red pines, eastern Hemlock, pitch pine
Wildlife	• muskrats, deer, gulls, copperhead snakes
Natural Resources	• soil: richest in river valleys in peat; products include cranberries, eggs, livestock, dairy products • minerals: sand and gravel in east-central region; some granite • 60% of state is forested

Vermont

Vegetation	• ash, basswood, beech, birch
Wildlife	• white-tailed deer, black bears, beavers
Natural Resources	• soil: richest in river valleys; products include maple syrup, dairy products, hay, timber, livestock • minerals: granite, marble, and talc in Green Mountains; marble and slate in Taconic Mountains • 75% of state is forested

Connecticut

Vegetation	• hemlock, mountain laurel, bayberry
Wildlife	• white-tailed deer, foxes, minks, trout
Natural Resources	• soil: at low elevations, soil is dry and crops such as tobacco are grown; land unsuitable for agriculture; products include apples, poultry, eggs • minerals: sand, gravel, and traprock; state does not depend on its own resources for manufacturing because it lacks large mineral deposits • 60% of state is forested

Rhode Island

Vegetation	• ash, birch, dogwood, fresh/seawater seaweed
Wildlife	• otters, screech owls, ruffed grouse
Natural Resources	• soil: richest along Narragansett Bay; products include potatoes, apples, milk, greenhouse/nursery products • minerals: limestone, sandstone, and westerly granite in the southwest used for building materials • 60% of state is forested

Sources: *World Book Encyclopedia,* 1991;
Quick Facts About the USA, Nancy Hartley, 1994;
1996 Information Please Almanac, Otto Johnson, editor, 1995

Geographic Regions of California

The Mountains

California has two major mountain ranges. The Sierra Nevada Range lines the state's eastern border. The Coastal Range is located along the western edge of the state. Logging and mining are the major industries. There are no large cities in these areas, but resort towns around Lake Tahoe in the Sierra Nevada and Yosemite National Park draw many tourists. Because of its elevation, snow and rainfall provide the area with water.

The Central Valley

The California Central Valley is located between the Sierra Nevada and the Coastal Range mountains. Cities such as Sacramento, Fresno, and Stockton have grown because of this rich agricultural area. The Sacramento River and the San Joaquin River provide water for crops.

The Deserts

The Mojave Desert and Death Valley are located in southeastern and southern California. Cities are scarce, but Palm Springs, situated near the Mojave Desert, is a major resort town. Some mining also takes place in this area. Water is provided by the Colorado River and Owens Lake, in the Sierra Nevada.

The Coast

The California Coast is the home to cities such as San Francisco, Los Angeles, and San Diego. These are located on the land between the Pacific Ocean and the Coastal Range. Industries of this area include fishing, oil/gas production, computers, and entertainment. Water is drawn from aqueducts stemming from the Sierra Nevada Range and Hoover Dam along the Arizona-Nevada border.

Source: *America the Beautiful: California*, R. Conrad Stein, 1988

The Midwest Flood of 1993

States Affected	North Dakota, South Dakota, Minnesota, Wisconsin, Iowa, Nebraska, Kansas, Illinois, Missouri
Major Rivers Involved	Iowa, Mississippi, Des Moines, Racoon, Missouri, Minnesota
Crops Destroyed	soybeans, corn, wheat, sorghum
Damages	• 17,000 square miles of land flooded • 48 people killed • 26,000 people evacuated • 59% less corn and soybeans harvested in the United States • 21,219 homes damaged
Relief	Red Cross provided: • shelters in schools and firehouses offering places to sleep • bottled water for drinking • portable toilets (without water service flushing is impossible) • flood relief centers providing prepared meals for those with no homes during the crisis which lasted 16 weeks; Approximately 2.5 million meals were served. • over $30 million in relief effort spending

Sources: *The Mississippi Flood,* Karin Luisa Badt, 1993

Where Crops are Grown in the United States

Crop	Where It Is Grown
Corn	Illinois, Indiana, Iowa, Michigan, Minnesota, Missouri, Nebraska, Ohio, South Dakota, Wisconsin
Soybeans	Illinois, Indiana, Iowa, Kansas, Minnesota, Missouri, Nebraska, Ohio
Wheat	Colorado, Kansas, Missouri, Montana, Nebraska, North Dakota, Oklahoma, South Dakota, Texas

Corn

Corn is used by	Uses
People	• sweet corn, popcorn, cereals, salad dressing, margarine, corn-starch, baby food, and corn syrup • corn meal (made from ground corn) found in cornbread, tamales, and tortillas
Livestock	• corn feed which is made of ground shelled corn, ground ears of corn, and chopped corn plants after the ear has been removed • animal feed
Industries	• ceramics, explosives, construction materials, metal molds, paints, paper goods, textiles • medicines such as penicillin, vitamins, and antibiotics • fuel

Soybeans

Soybeans are used by	Uses
People	• cooking oils, margarine, mayonnaise, salad dressing, ice cream, cosmetics, baby food, cereals, pet foods, insect sprays, spray paint, tofu, soy sauce, candles, soaps
Livestock	• animal feed
Industries	• adhesive tape, explosives, chemicals, textiles, fertilizer, disinfectants, fire extinguisher fluid, to provide firmness and protein in processed foods such as meats

Wheat

Wheat is used by	Uses
People	• flour, pasta, cereals, and bakery products
Livestock	• livestock feed made from wheat germ and bran which remains after the white flour is milled • animal bedding which comes from the wheat stalk (straw)
Industries	• fertilizers, synthetic rubber, glue, fuel • baskets and hats from woven straw

National Geographic Historical Atlas of the United States, 1993; *World Book Encyclopedia,* 1991

GLOSSARY

arid: dry

author: a person who gathers the data for a map

bay: part of a sea that is partly surrounded by land, smaller than a gulf

boroughs: small parts of the state of Alaska; many boroughs make up the state of Alaska

canal: a waterway built to carry water from one place to another

canyon: a deep valley with steep sides, usually with a stream running through it

census: a counting, which happens every ten years, of the people living in the United States

clear-cut: cutting that uses a giant sawing machine to strip entire hillsides of trees

coast: land along the sea

coastal plain: the flat stretch of land along a shore

continental divide: an imaginary line running along the Rocky Mountains that divides the rivers that flow east from the ones that flow west

conurbation: a system of interconnected cities and other areas, both urban and suburban

counties: small parts of a state; many counties make up one state

dam: a piece of land that holds back the flow of a body of water

date: tells when data for map was gathered

diversity: having many differences

earthquake: a sudden shaking or shock inside Earth that causes movement on its surface

ecosystem: a group of living organisms that depend on one another and the environment in which they live

elevation key: a part of a map that helps the reader understand the shape of the land

elevation/relief: the height of the land above sea level

erosion: the gradual wearing away of the earth

evaporate: to change to water vapor

fault: a fracture or break in Earth's crust

fragile: easily destroyed or damaged

glacier: a huge mass of ice that slowly slides down a mountain

globe: a model that represents Earth as it looks from space

gorge: a deep, narrow opening between steep and rocky sides of walls or mountains

grid: a system of longitude and latitude; helps find places on the map

harbor: a deep body of water where ships can anchor

human region: an area that might be defined by the characteristics of its people, such as their language or government

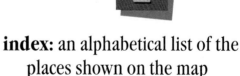

index: an alphabetical list of the places shown on the map

Intermontane region: the area between the Rocky Mountains and the Pacific Coastal Range

irrigation systems: systems of channels, streams, or pipes used to bring water to crops

legend: tells the meanings of the symbols on a map

mouth: the place where a river empties into a larger body of water

old-growth: vegetation that has existed for a long time

orientation: tells what direction things are from each other on the map

orographic precipitation: rain that occurs on only one side of a mountain or hill due to warm air being forced upward by the rise in land

physical region: an area of the natural landscape that might be defined by its landforms, plant and animal life, natural resources, or climate

political map: a map that shows boundary lines

population density: the amount of people per unit of land area

port: a place with a habor where ships can anchor

region: areas of land that share features that make them different from other areas; features may be physical or human

rural: in, of, or like the country

scale: shows the measurement of distances and areas

seedcut: cutting that leaves a few trees in an area to provide seeds for a new crop

selective cut: cutting that clears mature trees from an area to make room for new trees to grow

semi-desert: a dry area with very sparse vegetation, often located between a desert and a grassland

shelterwood cut: cutting that leaves a few trees in an area for other trees that need shade to grow

source: tells who provided the data for the map

sparse population: a small number of people spread out over a large area of land

title: tells what the map is supposed to show; the main idea of the map

urban: in, of, or like a city

valley: the lower land that lies between hills and mountains

volcano: an opening in Earth's crust from which ashes and hot gases flow

waterfall: a stream that flows over the edge of a cliff

watershed: all the water that drains from a land area into a creek, lake, or river

wetlands: areas that have wet soils, such as swamps and marshes